Andrea's Therapeutic Cooking Collection

Four Cookbooks in One! Recipes to Fight Cancer, Heart Disease and Build Your Immune System

Developed Life Books
4884 W. Hardy Rd
Tucson, AZ 85704
US

First Printing – 2016

Andrea's Therapeutic Cooking Collection

Contents

Introduction

Thank you a lot for buying this book! I hope it will assist with the incorporation of a diet that will rid you of so many threats to our health. This book is a collection of my series: **Andrea's Therapeutic Cooking**.

After you've done trying out these delicious recipes, please remember that a review on Amazon would really help me to keep going with all this.

Get My Books For Free!

If you bought this on Kindle for a couple of dollars (or on paperback for a few more) I greatly appreciate it. However, keep in mind you also have a chance to receive some of my products for free. This is by signing up to my mailing list. I will periodically run a free promotional tool, and I'll let my subscribers know whenever I do this.

In addition, everybody who signs up receives a FREE copy of my book: **The 20 Most Deceptive Health Foods**

The point of this book is to educate readers about what foods are actually healthy, and which ones are not.

It's a must-have to take with you to the grocery aisles.

You can join the exclusive mailing list right now at the following link:

http://www.developedlife.com/andreasilver.

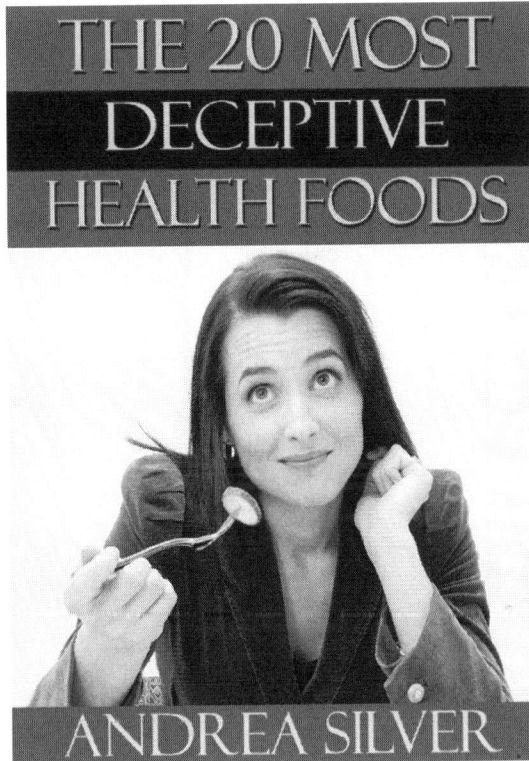

This is my completely free gift for my subscribers.

A Note About Measurements

I generally create these recipes using all or part of the metric system. This is more handy for exact measurements. There are many sites like metric-conversions.org where you can do conversions if you're not sure how to use metric or if you don't have a scale. If you are from the UK or USA and you are confused at all, go to this exact address: http://www.metric-conversions.org/volume/milliliters-to-us-cups.htm (this is for ml to US cups, as an example simply switch to UK cups or a different measurement that fits your country).

Through using ml this way for any type of recipe, you get exact amounts versus approximations.

Other Useful Recipe Books

I've also created recipe collections for "super foods" that can reinforce any type of healthy diet. You can check out:

My Turmeric Cookbook
(https://www.amazon.com/dp/B01AVY0EG4)

My Kale Cookbook
(https://www.amazon.com/dp/B01AVWG1WM)

My Salmon Cookbook
(https://www.amazon.com/dp/B01AI8RZCE)

My Hemp Cookbook
(https://www.amazon.com/dp/B01AX8486K

About this Cookbook Collection

Today, it's rare to hear a doctor tell a patient "Eat a great diet starting with these ingredients. Reduce the amount of stress in your life as much as you can, even if it means earning less money because your health is more important. Try some meditation, then call me and see how you feel." Instead it's usually "Pop these pills, call me when you need a refill." So more than ever it's important to prioritize nutrition.

For this collection, I'm targeting three areas of health that are extremely important: cancer prevention, heart health, and immune system building. Of course, as is often the case in nutrition, ingredients overlap and can be used to reinforce numerous areas of health. However, as I describe in the opening sections of each book, there are some ingredients more targeted than others. To tackle each area, you must have a solid strategy, which is what I provide to you.

What I've come to find is that by addressing all of these areas of health, it provides a lot of peace of mind. While sure, a potentially fatal disease can hit any of us, at anytime—it is great to know that you've reduced those chances as much as you can, while also maintaining overall health in every other area of your life. This means great benefit both psychologically and physiologically speaking.

Book One: Andrea's Cancer Fighting Cookbook

Andrea's
CANCER
FIGHTING
Cookbook

Carefully Selected Recipes to Prevent Cancer
and Become Healthier in General

ANDREA SILVER

Understanding a Cancer Prevention Diet

One thing agreed upon unanimously by oncologists is that cancer can, in many cases, be prevented, and a huge part of that involves your diet. That an increase in cancer is directly related to the failings of modern diets, and with a subject as terrifying as cancer, we can at least reassume a little bit of control by paying close attention to what we eat.

So that's where this cookbook comes into play. I've researched the different ingredients with proven links to cancer prevention, and compiled recipes, each tested by yours truly, that can make creating such a diet into something that's fun and exciting, with many new flavors to discover.

Now, clearly, there are many types of cancers, and many different causative factors. Unfortunately there is not, and never will be, a cancer cure-all strategy. But by remaining diligent with your diet, I do believe it's possible to up the odds greatly in your favor.

What I'm Not Offering

While oncologists agree that your diet has a huge factor in prevention (combined with other steps like avoiding toxin exposure and staying out of the sun), there is no agreement about whether your diet affects your odds after already being diagnosed with cancer. So, this cookbook is not about treating existing cancer, but preventing it.

This is where there is a lot of controversy. Mainstream school of thought is that what you eat has no effect on your survival rate. As an armchair critic, I don't necessarily agree with this point of view. I think it's a no-brainer that someone with cancer should be avoiding inflammatory, tumor-promoting white sugars, simple carbs, trans fats, red meats, etc.

At the same time, I don't necessarily buy the idea that you should forego all medical treatment and just eat a green detox diet as your sole method of curing yourself.

One website I quite like tells the story of a young man who opted for a detox diet instead of chemotherapy (while still undergoing surgery and radiation). It's called www.chrisbeatcancer.com. His opinions about this actually seem more balanced than some blogs / news sites that are more radical and less scientific.

I personally am unsure where I stand on this issue. I see the arguments from both sides and they each make valid points.

Cancer Prevention Basics

Firstly, it's important to combine what you eat with other areas, to ensure you are minimizing the risk as much as possible. Eating well while neglecting other important parts is counter-productive.

- Smoking

This is a no-brainer! Everybody knows smoking is linked to cancer. This is not something to mess around with, no matter how hard it is to quit.

- Obesity

Fortunately, a healthy cancer prevention diet, like the one outlined in this book, will also lead to weight loss. However, just eating right is never enough, because you also have to burn calories. I always suggest light to moderate weight-lifting daily for 30-60 minutes. Yes it takes discipline but obesity is a big causative factor.

- Toxin Exposure

Certain professions in particular make us more prone to cancers. Are you constantly exposed to industrial grade paints? Do you remodel old homes with asbestos risks? If your risk of cancer is high because of toxin exposure, it may be wise to even sacrifice your work for a new career.

- Alcohol

An occasional glass of wine or a beer won't kill you, but continued daily alcohol consumption increases your risk of various diseases, including cancers.

- Electromagnetic Exposure

Studies have shown excess cell phone use linked to cancer. There are also some concerns about WiFi signals coming from a connected phone. Long story short: get a headset if you're on the phone a lot.

- BPAs and BPS

These chemicals are found in plastics and can end up in your food and drinks. Experts suggest to find plastic containers with the recycling numbers 1, 2 or 4 to indicate BPA free.

- Excess Red Meat

Numerous studies have shown that continually eating red meat increases the risk of many of the deadliest cancers. While sometimes eating some red meat is good for you (B vitamins, etc), you don't want it in your diet every single day.

Dietary Basics

Here's the gist of this cookbook:

- Fiber

According to studies, every 10 grams of fiber added to your diet daily reduces the risk of colon by 10%. Good sources of fiber include leafy vegetables, whole wheat breads, and legumes.

- Ascorbic Acid

Ascorbic acid (vitamin C) has been linked to many cancer-fighting abilities. As a result, eating fruits like berries and tomatoes is an excellent way to boost this.

- Antioxidants

Antioxidants prevent the oxidization of your organs; improving organ health and your immune system among various factors. A better immune system means your body is running at great capacity to track and kill cancer cells. Antioxidant rich foods include pomegranate seeds, various berries like blueberry and acai, and green vegetables.

- Polyphenols

According to a 2007 study, polyphenols which are a class of antioxidant are directly related to the suppression of cancer cells[1]. One of the best sources is the spice turmeric.

- Healthy Fats

An important part of your cancer prevention diet is to remove all bad fats and replace them with body strengthening "good fats". Deep fried foods and margarines in particular contain "partially hydrogenated oil", which really means trans fat—a substance that raises the risk of many of the very deadly cancers. When cooking, use olive oil—or even better—coconut oil. Additional healthy fats and omega fatty acids can be found in nuts, avocados, and seeds like flax.

* * *

With all of that being said, let's move on to the recipes!

---

[1] http://www.ncbi.nlm.nih.gov/pubmed/17551696

Breakfast (Cancer Prevention)

Super Juice Blend

This is a special assortment of nutrients, including kale and beets. Very nutritious and a cornerstone of your cancer-fighting strategy.

Servings: 2

INGREDIENTS

- 2 large bunches organic kale leaves
- 2 large bunches organic silver beet leaves
- 1 medium organic green pear, chopped
- 1 medium organic green apple, chopped
- 1 large organic cucumber, chopped
- Juice of ½ organic lemon, freshly squeezed

DIRECTIONS

- In a blender, simply blend all the ingredients together. Serve cold.

Almond Blueberry Smoothie

A combination of the nutritious properties of almonds with the great antioxidant blueberry "superfood".

Servings: 2

INGREDIENTS

- 250 ml almond milk
- 225g almonds
- 750ml water
- 50g fresh organic blueberries
- 1 tsp vanilla beans

DIRECTIONS

- Simply blend all the ingredients together and pour into glasses. Serve cold.

Protein Banana Shake

Great if you are working out and putting on some muscle. There's some important ingredients here, including psyllium, flax seed and blueberries.

Servings: 2

INGREDIENTS

- 1 ripe banana
- Protein powder, put as much as you desire
- A handful or fresh organic blueberries
- 1 tbsp of psyllium seed husks
- 1 tbsp of flax seed oil
- 250ml soy milk

DIRECTIONS

Blend all the ingredients together, pour into glasses. Serve cold.

Turmeric Protein Shake

Turmeric is one of my favorite ingredients. Daily turmeric use has been linked to reduced rates of cancer and many inflammatory-related diseases.

Servings: 2

INGREDIENTS

Topping:

- 200ml organic orange juice, preferably homemade
- 2 tbsp soy protein powder
- 1 tsp turmeric powder
- 1 tsp vanilla seeds
- 250ml water

DIRECTIONS

- Blend all the ingredients together and pour into serving glasses. Serve immediately.

Broccoli and Seed Blend

The seeds contained in this recipe are some of the healthiest things you can eat. Add broccoli, and it' a nutrient powerhouse.

Servings: 2

INGREDIENTS

- 1 ripe banana
- 115g broccoli florets,
- 1 tsp grated ginger
- Juice of 1 organic lemon, freshly squeezed
- 12 mint leaves, washed
- 100g pomegranate arils
- 2 bunches washed kale leaves
- 225g organic strawberries
- 2 tbsp semi-sweet cocoa powder
- 2 tbsp flax seeds
- 1 tbsp chia seeds
- 25g hemp seeds
- 750ml water

DIRECTIONS

- Blend all the ingredients together. Serve immediately.

Carroty Lemonade

Vitamin C is a known cancer-fighter, and this is one of the best condensed sources of ascorbic acid.

Servings: 4

INGREDIENTS

- 450g organic carrots, washed and peeled
- 240 ml water
- 350ml organic sugar-free pineapple juice
- 200ml organic lemon juice, freshly squeezed
- Cold water
- Ice cubes
- Organic lemon wedges

DIRECTIONS

- In a pot, boil the water along with the carrots, allow it to simmer for 30 minutes.
- When the carrots are cooked through, place them aside to cool.
- Once the carrots are cool, blend them with the rest of the ingredients, except the ice cubes and lemon wedges, and chill in the fridge for about 3 hours. Serve with ice cubes and   lemon   wedges.

Raw Turmeric Tea

Soaking raw turmeric root creates a great tea. Add with a regular black tea bag if you wish.

Servings: 2

INGREDIENTS

- 750ml water
- 2 slices of turmeric root

DIRECTIONS

- In a pot over medium heat bring the water and turmeric to a boil and allow it to simmer for between 40 minutes to an hour. Cover and allow it sit overnight.
- Strain the turmeric out, leaving the liquid.
- Once ready to drink, reheat the turmeric water and you add some honey to sweetened it or perhaps drink it with your favorite tea.

Orange Blueberry Smoothie

Servings: 2

INGREDIENTS

- 1 orange segments
- 200g organic blueberries
- 120ml cold almond milk
- ½ ripe banana
- Ice cubes

DIRECTIONS

- Blend all the ingredients together and pour into glasses. Serve cold.

Broccoli Scrambled Eggs

Don't forget your greens in the morning. Here's a great way to integrate them. The recipe is also gourmet.

Servings: 1

INGREDIENTS

- 2 organic eggs
- 1 tsp water
- 1 tsp Parmesan cheese, grated
- Pinch of salt
- Pinch of black pepper, freshly grounded
- 1 tbsp extra-virgin olive oil
- 30g onion slices
- Pinch of dried thyme
- 50g broccoli

DIRECTIONS

- Whisk together the eggs, water, cheese, salt and pepper.
- In a non-stick pan, sauté the onions in the olive oil and add the thyme and broccoli. Stir until the broccoli is soft and cooked through. Add in the beaten eggs and scramble until it sets.

Gourmet Scrambled Eggs

Another good infusion of green veggies in the morning.

Servings: 1

INGREDIENTS

- 2 tbsp ghee
- 60g Brussels Sprouts, sliced
- ¼ onion. diced
- 50g mushrooms, sliced
- 4 eggs, beaten
- 1 tsp Dijon mustard
- ¼ tsp sea salt
- Pinch of black pepper, freshly grounded (optional)

DIRECTIONS

- In a non-stick skillet, heat the ghee and sauté the sprouts along with the onion and mushroom for about 9 minutes until soft. Add the mustard and seasoning.
- Add in the eggs and scramble until it sets.
- Serve immediately.

Quinoa Fruit Cereal Medley

A great assortment of seeds and super-foods.

Servings: 4

INGREDIENTS

- 150g quinoa, cooked
- 380ml almond milk
- 50g mixed dried fruits
- 1 cinnamon stick
- 4 tbsp honey
- ½ tsp cinnamon, grounded
- ¼ tsp cardamom
- Handful of fresh raspberries
- Handful dried currants
- Handful dried cranberries
- Pumpkin seeds
- Pomegranate seeds

DIRECTIONS

- In a saucepan over medium heat, add the cooked quinoa along with the milk, dried fruits and cinnamon. Cover and allow it to simmer for 10 minutes, while stirring occasionally. Discard the cinnamon stick and add in the honey and stir.
- Transfer to serving bowls, top with the rest of the ingredients. Serve warm.

Raspberry Beet Juice

This simple, bright red drink will leave friends wondering what the heck you're drinking.

Serving: 2

INGREDIENTS

- 6 beets, washed and chopped
- 400g fresh organic raspberries
- 1 inch ginger root, chopped

DIRECTIONS

- Blend all the ingredients together. Serve cold.

Lunch + Side Dishes (Cancer Prevention)

Cruciferous Avocado Salad

This salad is also great with some nuts or dried fruits.

Servings: 4

INGREDIENTS

- 280g carrots, shredded
- 280g cruciferous crunch salad mix, shredded
- 1 jalapeno, pitted and diced
- 400g chicken, cooked, shredded

Dressing:

- 1 large avocado
- 40g Greek yogurt
- 2 tsp lemon juice
- 1 tsp hot sauce
- 2 tbsp extra-virgin olive oil
- 2 tbsp water
- ¾ tsp garlic salt

DIRECTIONS

- In a bowl, toss together the salad ingredients.
- In another bowl, mix together the dressing ingredients.
- Place the salad into serving plate and top with the avocado dressing.

Grilled Avocado Bites

Avocados are a super food by themselves. This fresh salad is packed with alkalinity.

Serving: 1

INGREDIENTS

- 2 avocados, halved, thinly sliced bottom
- 1 tomato, cubed
- 1 tbsp fresh cilantro, roughly chopped
- 1 tbsp scallion, chopped finely
- 2 tsp finely chopped seeded jalapeno
- 1 tsp organic lime juice, freshly squeezed
- Extra-virgin olive oil
- ¼ tsp sea salt

DIRECTIONS

- In a bowl, mix the tomato, cilantro, scallion, jalapeno, lime juice and one teaspoon of oil olive along with a small pinch of salt.
- Heat your grill to high, meanwhile, brush the avocado with olive oil and grill until the grill marks appear. Transfer to serving plate and top with the tomato mixture.

Chicken Cranberry Sandwich

Cranberries are packed with nutrients. A great highly nutritious sandwich.

Serving: 4

INGREDIENTS

- 400g chicken, cooked and shredded
- 50g plain Greek yogurt
- 1 tbsp Dijon mustard
- ½ tsp sea salt
- ¼ tsp black pepper, freshly grounded
- 2 green onions, chopped
- 50g of mixed nuts
- 40g dried cranberries
- Handful of spinach leaves
- 4 100% stone ground whole wheat flour toast slices

DIRECTIONS

- In a bowl mix together all the ingredients.
- In a preheated toaster, grill the bread slices until golden and crisp. Spread the chicken mixture on two slices of toast and cover with the remaining slices.

Roasted Vegetable Galore

An impressive assortment of vegetables.

Serving: 4

INGREDIENTS

- 2 tomatoes, sliced in wedges
- 2 carrots, sliced
- 1 zucchini, sliced
- 1 red bell pepper, cubed
- 250g broccoli florets
- 1 red onion, sliced thinly
- 100g fresh corn kernels
- 2 tbsp avocado
- 35g fresh rosemary
- ¼ tsp red pepper flakes
- ¼ tsp sea salt
- 40ml balsamic vinegar
- 2 cloves garlic, crushed

DIRECTIONS

- Preheat the oven to 200 degree Celsius and prepare a baking sheet lined with parchment paper.
- In a bowl mix the vegetables together along with the avocado and using your hands, rub the vegetables together to ensure they are evenly coated. Add in the rest of the ingredients and mix to combine.
- Arrange the vegetable mixture onto the prepared baking sheet and sprinkle with 2 tablespoons of water. Roast in the preheated oven for 25 minutes, making sure to give them a toss occasionally. Serve hot.

Healthy Tabbouleh

For the classic recipe, use bulgur instead of quinoa.

Serving: 2

INGREDIENTS

- 50g spring onion, chopped
- 240g tomatoes, chopped
- 26g fresh mint, chopped
- 30g fresh parsley, chopped
- 1 lemon juice, freshly squeezed
- Extra virgin olive oil

DIRECTIONS

- Cook the quinoa as per instructions on the package. Fluff the quinoa with a fork and allow it to cool.
- In a bowl, mix the quinoa with the rest of the ingredients and stir to combine.

Kale Salad

This salad can also be served as a side dish.

Serving: 2

INGREDIENTS

Dressing:

- 60 ml grapeseed oil
- 80ml organic lemon juice, fresh squeezed
- 1 tbsp fresh ginger, grated
- 2 tsp whole grain mustard
- 2 tsp honey
- ¼ tsp salt

For the salad:

- 300g kale, thinly sliced from the spine
- 300g red cabbage, sliced
- 300g broccoli florets
- 2 large carrots, grated
- 1 red bell pepper, sliced
- 2 avocados, diced
- 50g fresh parsley, chopped
- 100g walnuts, roughly chopped
- 1 tbsp sesame seeds

DIRECTIONS

- First prepare the dressing, simply whisk all the dressing ingredients together and place aside until ready to serve.
- In a bowl, toss together the kale, cabbage, broccoli, bell pepper along with the carrots and transfer to serving plate.

Drizzle the desired amount of dressing over the salad and toss to combine.

- Top the salad parsley, avocado, sesame seeds and walnuts and give it a quick toss, and you're good to go.

Mango Avocado Salad

Mango and avocado makes for a great healthy combination of soft fruits.

Serving: 2

INGREDIENTS

- 700g arugula leaves
- 1 mango, sliced
- 1 avocado, sliced
- ½ red onion, chopped
- 1 tbsp lime juice, freshly squeezed

Vinaigrette:

- 1 tbsp apple cider vinegar
- ½ orange juice, freshly squeezed
- ½ lime juice, freshly squeezed
- 4 tbsp extra-virgin olive oil
- ½ tsp cumin powder
- 2 tbsp cilantro, finely chopped
- 1 red chili, sliced (optional)
- ¼ tsp sea salt
- ¼ tsp black pepper, freshly grounded

DIRECTIONS

- To make the dressing, place all the ingredients in a jar, lock it and give it a good shake.
- In some warm water with a pinch of salt add 1 tablespoon of lime juice, soak the sliced onions for 10 minutes.
- In a bowl, toss the arugula leaves and drizzle half of the dressing. Add in the avocado, mango and drained onions

and toss to combine. Transfer to serving plate, and drizzle the remaining dressing on top.

Apple Pomegranate Salad

You could use the dressing from the previous recipe to go on this basic but highly nutritious salad.

Serving: 2

INGREDIENTS

- 2 organic apples, sliced
- 1 package of spinach, washed
- 1 pomegranate
- 50g walnuts

DIRECTIONS

- Toss all the ingredients together in a bowl. Serve immediately.

Andrea's Power Guacamole

If you don't mind the spice, it's highly alkaline from the habanero, with great health benefits from the cilantro, pomegranate seeds, etc.

Serving: 4

INGREDIENTS

- 2 avocados, pitted and peeled
- 200g tomatillo pico de gallo
- 4 tsp habanero, chopped
- 400g pomegranate seeds
- Organic lemon juice, freshly squeezed
- Seas salt, to taste
- 50g queso fresco
- 250g tomatillo, diced
- 100g red onion, diced
- 30g cilantro, finely chopped

DIRECTIONS

- In a bowl toss together the avocados, pico de gallo, habanero and ¾ of the pomegranate along with some lemon juice and a pinch of salt. Mash with a fork until smooth.
- Transfer to serving bowl, and top with queso fresco along with the remaining pomegranate.

Garlic Potato Salad

Garlic has known cancer-fighting properties. The question is how we can introduce it into our diets. This potato salad is a great start.

Serving: 2

INGREDIENTS

- 3 potatoes, peeled and chopped
- 90g sweet peas
- 1 large carrot, peeled and sliced
- 2 cloves roasted garlic

Dressing:

- 100g plain Greek yogurt
- 1 tbsp low-fat mayonnaise
- 1 tbsp Dijon mustard
- 60ml apple cider vinegar

DIRECTIONS

- Steam your vegetables until soft and cooked through. Allow them to cool.
- Blend the dressing ingredients together.
- Remove bulbs from garlic cloves and dice into fine chunks and roast with a little bit of oil in a pan for a few minutes until soft. Add to mix.
- In a bowl, toss the cooled steamed vegetables with the dressing. Serve cold.

Stuffed Portabellos

This recipe is loaded with cancer-fighting alkaline properties.

Serving:4

INGREDIENTs

- 4 Portabello mushroom caps
- 4 potatoes, peeled and chopped
- 1 onion, diced
- 2 ripe tomatoes, diced
- 300g baby spinach, chopped
- 50g nutritional yeast
- 200g alfalfa sprouts
- 1 jalapenos, chopped
- 2 garlic cloves, crushed
- 1 tsp black pepper, freshly grounded
- Sea salt

DIRECTIONS

- Preheat the oven to 180 degree Celsius and line a baking sheet with parchment paper. Scrape out the centres of the Portabello caps.
- In a saucepan over medium heat, place the potatoes into cold water and bring to a boil. Lower the heat and allow it to simmer for 12 minutes then drain.
- In a bowl, using a fork, mash the potatoes with the onion, tomatoes, spinach, yeast, jalapeno, garlic and the spices.
- Fill the mushroom caps with the potato mixture. Bake for 25 to 30 minutes until the Portabello is tender. Garnish with the alfalfa sprouts and serve warm.

Pomegranate Salad

If you're not vegetarian, I like to load this flavorful salad up with some chicken, as well.

Serving: 4

INGREDIENTS

- 500 g fresh kale, washed and chopped
- 1 clove garlic, minced
- ¼ tsp black pepper, freshly grounded
- ¼ tsp sea salt
- 1 lemon
- 2 tbsp extra-virgin olive oil
- 1 tsp honey
- 1 handful mint, chopped
- 1 handful parsley, chopped
- 2 tbsp seeds (pumpkin seeds for example)
- 1 pomegranate
- 2 tbsp dried cranberries
- 50g walnuts

DIRECTIONS

- In a bowl, whisk together the garlic, pepper, lemon juice, olive oil and honey. Pour onto the kale leaves and toss to evenly coat the leaves.
- Transfer to serving bowl, and top with the herbs, seeds, pomegranates, cranberries and walnuts. Serve immediately.

Crunchy Veggies

Sweet potato also works well instead of the veggies.

Servings: 2

INGREDIENTS

- 1 package Brussels sprouts
- 1 onion, chopped
- 4 celery stalks, chopped
- 2 carrots, sliced
- 4 garlic cloves, minced
- 50ml grape-seed oil
- ¼ tsp sea salt

DIRECTIONS

- Preheat your oven to 200 degree Celsius and line a baking sheet with parchment paper.
- In bowl, toss together all the ingredients.
- Bake for 25 to 30 minutes until the desired level of crunchiness of the vegetables is reached. Serve warm.

Roasted Squash

You can serve this as a side dish, or as a meal

Serving: 2-4

INGREDIENTS

- ½ kg butternut squash, peeled and cubed
- ½ kg golden beets, peeled and sliced
- 2 ½ tbsp sesame oil
- 2 tbsp tahini
- 1 tbsp organic lemon juice, freshly squeezed
- 2 tsp fresh oregano leaves, chopped
- 1 tsp fresh rosemary, chopped
- ½ tsp sea salt
- ¼ tsp cracked black pepper
- 2 tbsp shelled, raw pistachios

DIRECTIONS

- Preheat the oven to 200 degree Celsius. Prepare your baking sheet lined with parchment paper.
- In a bowl, toss together all of the ingredients, excluding the pistachios. Arrange in a single layer on the prepared baking sheet and roast for about 20 minutes, rotate the baking sheet halfway through. Add in pistachios and roast for additional 5 minutes. Serve warm.

Roasted Butternut Squash with Pears

For an extra crunch, feel free to toss in some nuts. This is a good combination of healthy fruits and vegetables.

Serving: 4

INGREDIENTS

- 16 Brussels sprouts, washed
- 1 pear, cored and cubed
- 1 small butternut squash, peeled and cubed
- 3 tbsp extra-virgin olive oil
- Pinch of sea salt
- Pinch of black pepper, freshly grounded

DIRECTIONS

- Preheat the oven to 200 degree Celsius. Prepare a Pyrex baking dish.
- In a bowl, toss all the ingredients together and arrange them into the prepared baking dish.
- Bake for 35 to 40 minutes until soft and lightly browned. Serve warm.

Spiced Stuffed Onions

This recipe is great with some tabbouleh,
Yield: 10

INGREDIENTS

- 3 large onions, opened from the centre, top to bottom
- 250g white rice, soaked in water
- 1 tbsp tomato paste
- 2 tsp cinnamon
- 1 tsp allspice
- 1 tsp cumin, grounded
- 1 tsp coriander, grounded
- 1 1/2 tsp sea salt
- Pinch of black pepper, freshly grounded
- 3 tbsp parsley, chopped, plus extra for garnish
- 2 tbsp apple cider vinegar
- 1 tsp sugar
- 2 tbsp extra-virgin olive oil

DIRECTIONS

- In a pot, fill it with water, enough to cover more than the whole onion and bring it to a boil. When the water boils, add in the onions and cook for 10 minutes. Drain the rice.
- In a large bowl, add the rice, paste, spices, salt, pepper and parsley and mix to combine. Drain the onions and allow them to cool.
- Stuff each onion with a heaping tablespoon of the filling. In a pan, heat the olive oil and sauté the onions for 3 minutes until the bottoms are lightly browned, then add in the vinegar and sprinkle ¼ sugar on the onions. Lower the heat and cover, cook for 20 minutes until cooked through. Serve immediately.

Roasted Cauliflower Salad

This salad is packed with anti-cancer phytochemicals.

Serving:4

INGREDIENTS

- ¾ kg cauliflower
- 60ml extra virgin olive oil
- 2 celery stalk, sliced
- 5 tbsp walnuts
- 5 tbsp hazelnut
- 5 tbsp pecans
- 30g parsley, chopped
- 30g fresh mint, chopped
- ½ pomegranate seeds
- ½ tsp cinnamon
- ½ tsp coriander seed, grounded
- ¼ tsp nutmeg, grounded
- 1 tbsp apple cider vinegar
- 1 tsp honey
- Pinch of sea salt
- Pinch of black pepper, freshly grounded

DIRECTIONS

- Preheat oven to 220 degree Celsius and prepare a baking dish.
- In a bowl, toss together the cauliflower with 3 tablespoons of olive oil along with a pinch of salt and pepper. Arrange in the prepared baking dish and roast for 25 minutes until golden and cooked through. Transfer to a bowl and set aside to cool.
- Lower the oven temperature to 162 degree Celsius and place the nuts onto a baking sheet lined with parchment

paper and toast in the oven for 10 minutes. Place aside to cool then chop them up.

- Add the chopped nuts to the cooled cauliflower along with the remaining ingredients and toss to combine. Adjust seasoning and serve at room temperature

Dinner + Side-Dishes (Cancer Prevention)

With ingredients like turmeric, cumin, tahini, and greens—this is about as healthy as it gets.

Andrea's Spicy Coleslaw

Servings: 4-6

INGREDIENTS

- 300g red cabbage, shredded
- 300g green cabbage, shredded
- 1 fennel bulb, shredded
- 1 small red onion, sliced thinly
- 1 carrot, grated
- 50g raisins
- 1 apple, diced
- Pinch of sea salt
- Pinch of black pepper, freshly grounded
- 100g plain Greek Yogurt

- 2 tbsp extra-virgin olive oil
- 2 garlic cloves, minced
- 1 tbsp raw brown sugar
- 1 lemon juice, freshly squeezed
- 1 tsp cumin
- 1 tbsp turmeric
- 2 tbsp tahini
- 1 tbsp celery seed

DIRECTIONS

- In a bowl, mix together the two cabbages, fennel, onion, carrot, raisin, apple and salt and pepper.
- In another bowl, whisk all the remaining ingredients and pour over the slaw and mix well to combine. Keep in the fridge until ready to serve.

Spanish Rice

A rice dish without rice!

Serving: 4

INGREDIENTS

- 1 avocado, peeled and mashed
- 1 tsp chili powder (optional)
- 2 tsp paprika
- ½ tsp curcumin
- ½ tsp onion powder or 2 tbsp chopped onion
- 1 tsp salt
- Pinch of black pepper
- 1 head cauliflower
- 1 red bell pepper, diced
- 2 tomatoes, diced
- 3 scallions, sliced
- 25g cilantro leaves, chopped
- 2 tsp fresh basil, chopped
- 1 clove garlic, crushed
- 4 tsp lemon juice, freshly squeezed
- 60ml extra virgin olive oil
- 1 tbsp honey

DIRECTIONS

- In a bowl, mix the avocado with the seasoning.
- In a food processor, blend the cauliflower until it becomes like a rice consistency. Transfer to a bowl then add in the avocado and the rest of the ingredients and serve.

Butternut Squash Soup

Serving: 4

INGREDIENTS

- 2.3 litres organic chicken broth
- 340g butternut squash, cubed
- 1 small onion
- 6 stalks celery, chopped
- 6 carrots, chopped
- Pinch of sea salt
- Black pepper, freshly grounded
- Organic lemon juice, freshly squeezed
- 5 cloves garlic, crushed
- 100g green cabbage, chopped
- 60ml apple cider vinegar

DIRECTIONS

- In a deep pot cook the broth with the celery, carrots and onions, let it simmer until the desired flavor and consistency is reached. Adjust seasoning. Allow the broth to cool down. Add the raw garlic to the broth.
- In a food processor blend the broth which cooled down.
- Squash and add in the cabbage and return on heat bring t to a boil. Adjust seasoning and add in vinegar, lemon juice and any cruciferous raw vegetables and pour into serving bowls and serve hot.

Roasted Turmeric Vegetables

You can add some dried raisins to this dish, too.

Serving:2

INGREDIENTS

- 1 head of cauliflower
- 6 shallots, whole and peeled
- 250g cherry tomatoes, washed and halved
- 400g cannellini beans, rinsed
- 3 bay leaves
- 120ml water
- 60ml extra virgin olive oil
- 1 tbsp organic lemon juice, freshly squeezed
- 2 tsp turmeric, grounded
- 1 tsp nigella seeds
- ½ tsp sweet paprika
- ¼ tsp cumin powder
- Sea salt
- Black pepper, freshly grounded
- 50g parsley, finely chopped

DIRECTIONS

- Preheat oven to 170 degree Celsius and prepare a baking dish. In a bowl, toss together the vegetables and the bay leaves. In another bowl, whisk together the water, oil, lemon juice, turmeric, nigella seeds, paprika, cumin, salt and pepper. Pour over the vegetabled and toss to combine.
- Arrange the vegetables into the baking dish and roast for an hour in the preheated oven until the vegetables are cooked through and the cauliflower become golden. Place onto serving plate and top with chopped parsley and serve.

Whole Grain Pasta Galore

In moderation, eating pasta is just fine—especially if it's whole grain.

Serving:6

INGREDIENTS

- 2 tbsp plus 2 additional tsp extra virgin olive oil
- ¼ kg whole grain macaroni shells
- 1 large broccoli crown, broken
- 2 tbsp shallot, finely chopped
- 2 tbsp flour, sifted
- 720ml milk
- Pinch of sea salt
- Pinch of black pepper, freshly grounded
- Pinch of nutmeg
- 100g grated Gruyère
- 28g Parmesan, freshly grated

DIRECTIONS

- Heat oven to 180 degrees Celsius and spray a baking dish with oil. In a large pot of water with 12 teaspoons of salt, cook the pasta until just cooked through but not too soft. Drain but reserve the water and place into a bowl and add 1 tablespoon of oil and mix together.
- Cook for another 3 minutes, drain , place into a bowl of cold water to stop the cooking process and drain again then pat dry with a paper towel.
- In a saucepan heat 2 tablespoons of oil and add in the shallots and sauté for 3 minutes. Stir in the flour and cook until it bubbles, be careful not to brown it. Use a whisk and mix in the milk constantly until it begins to thicken.

- Lower the heat and allow it simmer while you stir, for 15 minutes until the flour is cooked through and until the sauce is thick and smooth.
- Adjust seasoning and remove from the heat. Pour the sauce into a bowl while it is still hot and add in the broccoli and pasta and toss to evenly coat.
- Transfer to the prepared baking dish and bake for 35 to 40 minutes until lightly golden on top. Allow it to rest for 10 minutes and serve.

  .

Classic Lentil Soup

Serving: 6

INGREDIENTS

- 1 onion, chopped
- 3 tbsp extra-virgin olive oil
- 2 medium carrots, chopped
- 2 stalks celery, chopped
- 2 cloves garlic, crushed
- 1 bay leaf
- 2 tomatoes, chopped
- 250g dry lentils
- 2 litres low-sodium vegetable broth
- 60g spinach, chopped
- ¼ tsp turmeric, grounded
- 1/8 tsp black pepper, freshly grounded

DIRECTIONS

- In a large pot over medium heat, heat the oil and add in the onions, carrots, and celery and sauté for 3 minutes. Add the garlic and once the onion are soft, pour in the broth and the bay leaves, and cook for 3 minutes. Toss in the lentils and tomatoes and bring soup to a boil. Lower the heat and allow it to simmer for an hour, add in the spinach and cook, adjust the seasoning. Pour into serving bowls and serve warm.

Turmeric Soup

Serving: 4

INGREDIENTS

- 200g pumpkin (canned or fresh), chopped
- 4 carrots, chopped
- 1 sweet potato, chopped
- 4 tomatoes, chopped
- 3 cloves garlic, crushed
- 1tsp mustard seeds
- 1 onion, chopped
- 300ml vegetable broth
- 200ml coconut milk
- 1 handful of fresh cilantro, chopped
- Fresh turmeric root, about a 5cm piece, chopped
- Ginger root, 5cm piece, chopped
- ½ bell pepper, chopped
- 100g of organic lentils
- Drizzle of coconut oil
- 75g cashews, roughly chopped
- 2 tbsp pepitas
- 1 clove garlic, crushed
- Red chili (optional)

DIRECTIONS

- In a pot heat some extra virgin olive oil and toss in the turmeric, ginger, seeds and garlic and stir. Add in the carrot, pumpkin, potato, pepper and the tomatoes and stir.
- Pour in the broth and add in the lentils. Lower the heat and allow the soup to simmer until the vegetables and lentils are cooked through.
- Remove from the heat, using a handheld blender, blend the soup until smooth and add the coconut milk and cilantro and blend until the desired thickness is reached.

- In a pan, heat some coconut oil and toast the cashews with the pepitas and garlic until golden. Pour the soup into serving bowls and top with some of the cashew topping.

Kale Stew

It tastes better than it sounds!

Serving: 4

INGREDIENTS

- 1 bunch kale, trimmed
- 2 tomatoes, chopped
- 1 onion, finely chopped
- 5 cloves garlic, minced
- 240ml water, may require more
- 4 tsp extra-virgin olive oil
- A small pinch of saffron threads
- ¾ tbsp sweet paprika
- ¼ tsp coriander, grounded
- ¼ tsp cumin seed (may substitute ground cumin)
- Pinch ground cloves
- 420g chickpeas
- 1/2 teaspoon salt, or more to taste
- 2 tbsp lemon juice, freshly squeezed
- 3 tbsp fresh cilantro, roughly chopped

DIRECTIONS

- In a pot, bring the water to a boil and add in the kale, cook until wilted, then drain without squeezing it. In a pan over medium heat, heat the oil and add in the onion, garlic, tomatoes and stir for 5 minutes.
- Add in the saffron then the paprika, coriander, cumin, and stir for 2 minutes.
- Add in the chickpeas with 120ml water, increase the heat and bring it to a boil. Add in the kale and salt, lower the heat and let it simmer for 10 minutes stirring occasionally.

- Do not let the stew bubble or else it will lose its consistency. Add in the lemon juice and cilantro. Pour into serving bowls and serve hot

Broccoli Soup

A delicious detox soup.

Serving: 2

INGREDIENTS

- 300g broccoli florets
- 2 celery stalks, diced
- 1 onion, chopped
- 2 garlic cloves, minced
- 250g spinach, washed
- 1 parsnip, peeled and chopped
- 1 medium carrot, chopped
- 380ml vegetable broth
- ¼ tsp sea salt
- Juice of ½ organic lemon., freshly squeezed
- ½ tbsp coconut oil
- 2 tsp chia seeds
- Handful of nuts of your choice, toasted
- ½ tbsp coconut milk

DIRECTIONS

- In a pot, heat the coconut oil and add the onion, garlic, carrot, parsnip, celery, broccoli and stir fir 5 minutes. Pour in the broth, cover and allow the soup to simmer for 7 minutes until the vegetables are tender. Toss in the spinach.
- Remove from the heat, add in the chia and lemon juice and using a handheld blender, blend the soup until smooth. Pour into serving bowls and top with the toasted nuts and a drizzle of coconut milk.

Spinach Cauliflower Tagine

Serving: 2

INGREDIENTS

- 1 head of cauliflower, broken into small pieces
- 1 turnip, diced
- 1 carrot, diced
- 1 clove garlic, minced
- 1 shallot, chopped finely
- 2 dried apricots, chopped
- 2 dates, chopped
- 4 leaves kale, roughly chopped
- 30g pine nuts
- 3 tbsp extra-virgin olive oil
- 2 tsp nama shoyu
- 2 tsp tamarind, presoaked and strained
- 1 tbsp cumin seeds
- 1 tbsp coriander
- 2 tsp fresh turmeric root
- 2 tsp fresh cilantro, chopped
- 2 tsp fresh mint, chopped
- 1 jalapeno, chopped (optional)

DIRECTIONS

- Preheat the oven to 160 degree Celsius, prepare a baking dish. In a bowl, toss together the cauliflower, turnip, carrot, garlic, shallot, apricot, dates and kale. Pour in the olive oil and add in the nama shoyu and tamarind. Add the spices and cilantro and stir to combine.
- Transfer to the prepared baking dish and cook in the oven for about an hour. Serve warm.

Mushroom Soup

You can add some cruciferous greens to this soup

Serving: 4

INGREDIENTS

- 200g dried split peas
- 1 liter of water
- 4 onions, tops sliced off and peeled
- 4 zucchinis, peeled
- 3 leeks, washed, bottoms cut and sliced
- 2 bunches of broccoli
- 2kg carrots, peeled and juiced
- 2 heads of celery, trimmed and juiced
- 120g raw unsalted cashews
- 450 g mushrooms, cleaned and sliced
- 1 tbsp granulated garlic powder
- 2 bay leaves
- 1 tsp sea salt

DIRECTIONS

- In a pot add the water and peas and bring to a boil and add in the onions. Lower the heat and let it simmer. Add in the zucchinis and leeks and cover.
- Add the carrot and celery juices and stir. Scoop some of the soup to a food processor with the onions, zucchinis and leeks, leaving the peas in the pot; blend until smooth. Add the cashew and more of the soup and blend together.
- Finish blending the rest of the soup and return back to the pot and add the mushrooms and bay leaves. Allow the soup to simmer for about 20 more minutes until the mushrooms are tender. Season with salt and garlic powder, discard the bay leaves and serve hot.

Leek Soup

Roast some slices of whole grain bread to go with this soup.

Serving: 4-6

INGREDIENTS

- 25g unsalted butter
- 2 leeks, chopped
- 1 garlic clove, minced
- 2 tsp dried sage
- 1 head broccoli, broken into florets
- 1 litre vegetable broth
- Some grated Cheddar, to garnish

DIRECTIONS

- In a pot over medium heat, melt the butter and stir in the leeks and a pinch of sea salt. Cover and let it cook for 5 minutes until the leeks are tender. Add in the garlic, sage, broccoli, broth and allow it to simmer for 15 minutes until the broccoli if cooked through. Remove the pot from the heat and allow it to cool for a few minutes.
- Using a handheld blender, blend the soup until smooth and creamy. Pour into serving bowls and top with some grated Cheddar.

Lemony Roasted Sprouts

Serving: 2

INGREDIENTS

- 1 large organic lemon, zested and juiced
- 1 tbsp unsalted butter
- ½ kg Brussels sprouts, trimmed and halved in half
- ¼ tsp salt
- 2 tsp apple cider vinegar

DIRECTIONS

- Preheat the oven to 200 degree Celsius. Spray a baking pan with cooking spray. Place the pan on medium heat and melt in the butter, then add in the sprouts and sprinkle with salt. Lower the heat and cook the sprouts for 6 minutes until browned.
- Add in the lemon zest and juice along with the vinegar and stir. Place the pan into the preheated oven and bake for 6 minutes until the sprouts are tender. Serve hot.

Chicken & Rice Turmeric Blend

You have to give me credit, most of my recipes are vegetarian or even vegan friendly… Just not this one.

Serving: 2

INGREDIENTS

- 3 tbsp olive oil
- 1 garlic clove, minced
- 4 chicken drumsticks, skins removed
- 1 tbsp ground turmeric
- 230g white rice
- 1 carrot, chopped
- 250g canned chickpeas
  Pinch of sea salt

DIRECTIONS

- In a pot over medium heat, heat the olive oil and stir in the garlic. Stir for a minute then remove the garlic. Add in the chicken and turmeric and cook for 4 minutes until golden brown on all sides. Pour water into the pan until the chickens are covered and cook for 20 minutes making sure that you stir occasionally.
- Stir in the rice, carrots, chickpeas and cover again with more water. Lower the heat, cover and bring to a boil. Adjust seasoning and cook until all the water is absorbed. Remove from the heat and let it stand for 15 minutes.

Grand Vegetable Soup

The motherload of vegetables. This is Southeast Asian inspired.

Serving: 6

INGREDIENTS

- 3 tbsp coconut oil
- 2 onions, sliced
- 1 head of bok choy, separated, washed and diced
- 4 cloves garlic, crushed
- ⅓ large head cabbage , shredded
- 2 carrots, diced
- Ginger root, grated
- 500g spinach
- 1.5 liters beef broth (optional)
- 1 tsp sea salt
- ½ tsp black pepper, freshly grounded
- 10 artichoke hearts, chopped
- 350g cooked beef (optional)
- 250g broccoli, chopped
- 200g cauliflower, chopped
- 350g water chestnuts, drained and sliced
- Dash of soy sauce
- Parmesan, grated, to garnish

DIRECTIONS

- In a pot over medium heat, heat the coconut oil and sauté the onions in it, stir for 5 minutes then add in the garlic.
- Wash the bok choy well and dice the woody white parts off the stems.
- Add the bok choy to the onions. Add the cabbage, carrots, garlic and ginger and stir. Then add the spinach. Stir until the green are wilted.

- Pour in the broth and increase the heat, adjust seasoning and add the black pepper, paprika, artichokes and the cooked meat. Cover and bring to a boil.
- Add the broccoli, cauliflower and water chestnuts. When the soup comes to a boil, lower the heat and simmer for 15 minutes.
- When the vegetables are tender, pour soup into serving bowls and serve with soy sauce and garnish with grated parmesan.

Vegetable Frittata

Serving: 6

INGREDIENTS

- 3 bell peppers, seeded and quartered
- 4 garlic cloves
- 2 large zucchini, sliced
- 30g fresh parsley, chopped
- 1 tsp salt
- 4 organic eggs
- 6 organic egg whites
- ¼ tsp cayenne pepper
- 60g grated Parmesan
- 1 onion, sliced
- 1 tbsp extra-virgin olive oil

DIRECTIONS

- Preheat the oven to 220 degree Celsius and prepare two baking sheets lined with foil sprayed with cooking oil. Arrange the oven racks to one in the centre and one in the lowest rack.
- In a pan over medium heat, cook the peppers with the garlic and zucchini and onion and add some olive oil. Place bell peppers and garlic in one pan and zucchini and onion in the other.
- Arrange the onion and zucchini on the baking sheet that will go on the lowest rack and the peppers and garlic on the centre rack and roast for 10 minutes. Remove from the oven and carefully remove the skin of the peppers and garlic and transfer the roasted vegetables to a bowl.
- Add in the parsley and a pinch of salt and toss to combine.
- Lower the oven temperature to 180 degree Celsius and prepare a cake pan sprayed with cooking oil. In a bowl, whisk the eggs then whisk in the egg whites, add a pinch of

salt, cayenne pepper and parmesan then pour into the prepared cake tin. Bake uncovered for 40 to 50 minutes and allow it to stand for 5 minutes before serving.

Desserts Aren't Always Bad For You (Cancer Prevention)

Chocolate Apple Bites

Servings: 6

INGREDIENTS

- 2 apples, cut into wedges
- 40g crunchy peanut butter
- 50g granola
- ¼ tsp cinnamon, grounded
- Handful of semi-sweet chocolate chips

DIRECTIONS

- Spread the peanut butter onto the apple wedges and coat with granola and cinnamon. Pour the chocolate chips in glass and melt in the microwave. Drizzle the melted chocolate over the wedges and serve.

Vanilla Bean Yogurt

This yogurt is great with granola

Serving: 2

INGREDIENTS

- 2 coconuts, flesh scooped out, rinsed and blended (reserve the water)
- 1/2 vanilla bean pod, scraped
- ½ tbsp coconut nectar
- 5 drops stevia
- ½ organic lemon juice, freshly squeezed

DIRECTIONS

- Blend the rinsed coconut flesh and add to it half of the coconut water. Add inn the rest of the ingredients and blend at low speed until smooth. Serve with a handful of fresh berries of your choice.

Chocolate Bean Cake

Seems an unusual combination, but remember that chocolate is a bean, too! This cake is high in fiber, an important part of a cancer-prevention strategy.

Serving: 4

INGREDIENTS

- 400g black beans, cooked
- 4 large organic eggs
- 2 tsp mint extract
- ½ tbsp stevia
- 50ml canola oil
- 70ml honey
- 75g unsweetened dark cocoa powder
- 1 ½ tsp baking powder
- ¾ tsp baking soda
- Pinch of salt
- Fresh mint leaves, for garnish

DIRECTIONS

- Preheat oven to 175 degree Celsius and prepare a baking tin with parchment paper. Blend together the beans, half the eggs, oil, honey and mint until smooth.
- In a bowl sift together the dry ingredients.
- In another bowl beat the eggs and pour the bean mixture into the beaten eggs and stir. Add in the dry ingredients and mix with a wooden spoon until smooth. Transfer to baking tin and bake in the preheated oven for 30 to 40 minutes until a toothpick inserted comes out clean.

Healthy Muffins

Serving: 4

INGREDIENTS

- 150g whole wheat flour
- 30g light brown sugar
- 1 tsp baking powder
- 50g pecans, roughly chopped
- ½ tsp salt
- 200g blueberries
- 60ml almond milk
- 1 large organic egg

DIRECTIONS

- Preheat oven to 180 degree Celsius and prepare a baking sheet lined with muffin cups.
- Sift together the dry ingredients except the sugar. In another bowl, beat the sugar with the eggs then add the milk. Slowly add in the dry ingredients to the egg mixture and mix using a wooden spoon until smooth. Pour into the muffin cups and bake for 35 minutes or until a toothpick inserted comes out clean.

Antioxidant Layered Granola Parfait

Serving: 2

INGREDIENTS

- 200g strawberries, halved
- 100 g pomegranate seeds
- 100 g acai berries
- 170g vanilla yogurt
- 30g granola

DIRECTIONS

- Layer the ingredients in the desired order into the serving cups and serve cold.

Almond Chia Pudding

We've come to the end of this book. I'll leave you with some chia seed pudding, something I never thought was possible before I started experimenting with recipe combinatins.

Serving: 2

INGREDIENTS

- 4 tbsp chia seeds
- 240ml of almond milk
- 1 tsp vanilla extract
- 1 tbsp organic honey
- ¼ tsp salt

DIRECTIONS

- In a bowl combine all the ingredients together and allow it to sit, covered, for 7 hours or overnight making sure that you stir occasionally.
- Transfer the pudding to serving cups and top with fresh berries.

Book Two: Andrea's Heart Healthy Cookbook

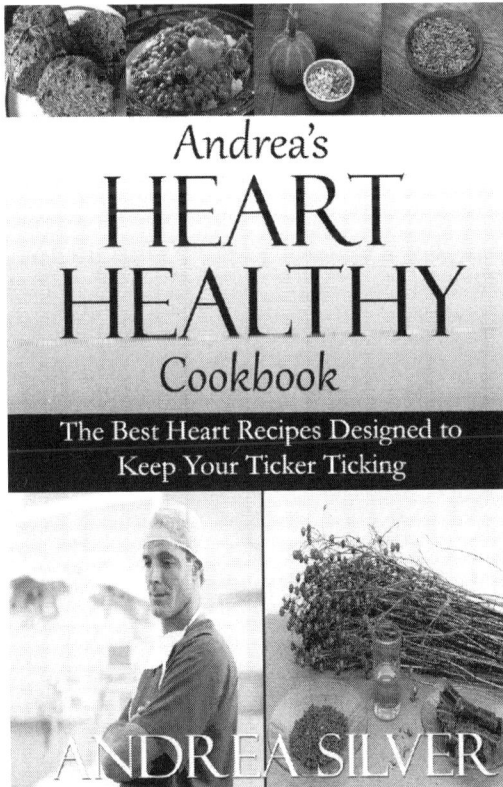

Getting Started With a Heart Healthy Diet

As heart disease is the leading cause of death, it makes sense for everyone to consider their heart as one of the most important aspects of their diets.

Fortunately, anybody who reads my books—in particular my cookbooks—will automatically be helping their hearts. Many ingredients, including "super foods" that I advocate—from avocado to kale to hemp—are beneficial for your heart. In this way, your health is not as complex as you may think—because many ingredients synergize together to provide optimal health to you.

However, there may also come a time to focus especially on just one area—in this case, the heart. There are some reason to consider doing this: if heart disease runs in your family, if you've suffered a heart attack in the past, if your doctor recommends it, if you are 65 years or older, or if you just want the confidence of knowing your ticker is in good shape.

So I am now presenting an assortment of recipes utilizing foods rich in omega oils, antioxidants, and proven heart healthy compounds. Some of these heart mega-foods include:

- Flax seed
- Pumpkin
- Nuts like almonds
- Coconut
- Oatmeal (or porridge, if you're a UK reader! My UK friend says 'oatmeal' sounds like something you feed to horses.)
- Lots of whole grains
- Quinoa
- And plenty of fruits and vegetables

All of these recipes are vegetarian friendly, and tested by yours truly to ensure they're quality and taste good. Some recipes are inspired from other recipes I've found, but each one I customize a bit so it's original and has a bit of my own flare attached to it. I hope you enjoy them.

Some Basics About Your Heart Healthy Diet

Regardless of what recipes you choose to incorporate into your diet, here are some basic 'rules' for rejuvenating your heart.

- Always choose whole grains over white breads or pastas. Even better, use healthy quinoa instead of white rice or pasta. Gummy white carbs are bad for your heart, while whole grain, fibrous foods are good for your heart.

- Avoid unhealthy fats. This includes saturated fat and trans-fat. One of the most common ways we consume these fats is when we buy "healthy" butter spreads—AKA margarines—which are really anything but healthy!

- Avoid over-frying your food. This can create unhealthy fats. A quick stir-fry in healthy oil (like coconut oil) is fine, but keeping a slice of bacon on a skillet for ten minutes is bad news!

- Make sure you eat green food every-day. As every doctor in the world says, don't neglect your vegetables. They contain the needed nutrients to maintain heart health.

- We know cholesterol buildup can clog your arteries. However, new health science is finding how the bigger threat is actually inflammation—as bodily / internal inflammatory states precipitate the artery clogging (as well as other diseases). Therefore, avoid foods that cause inflammation—such as lots of sugar, any kind of soda pop, (again) white breads, etc.

A Note About Stress

Your mind and body are linked to each other. If you are prone to episodes of panic, anger, fear or other high blood-pressure inducing emotions throughout the day, this could be greatly increasing your risk of not only heart attack, but also various other diseases, including strokes!

It may be critically important to take up daily meditation. Learn to clear your mind and induce feelings of calmness in any situation. When you can master this, you won't have to worry about your emotions compromising your health. This is every bit as important as the foods you are eating. It's almost pointless to pursue one without the other.

It Gets Easier As You Go

Meditating and switching from spaghetti to quinoa sounds great on paper, but actually changing your habits is hard for anyone to do.

However, lifestyle changes are easier when you begin to enjoy the pleasures of it, and then you won't want to turn back. For instance, if you follow the recipes in this book consistently, you'll find that ou have improved energy and digestion.

Once you're living those benefits, it becomes much easier to stay true to your diet because you won't want to turn back!
Alright! Now that you understand the basics of a heart healthy diet, let's move on to the recipes.

Enjoy!

Breakfast (Heart Healthy Cookbook)

Whole Grain Fruit Bowl

You can use a variety of fruits in this recipe.

Servings: 2

INGREDIENTS

- 185g cooked red quinoa
- 100g cooked barley
- 50g fresh blueberries
- 100g strawberries, thinly sliced
- 175g apple, sliced
- 200g mandarin oranges
- 1 banana, thinly sliced
- 70g unsalted walnuts, roughly chopped

Dressing:

- 100ml flax oil
- 50 ml olive oil
- 70ml organic honey
- 150ml golden balsamic vinegar
- 1 tsp cinnamon, grounded
- 1/4 tsp nutmeg, grounded
- 1 tbsp gingcr, freshly grated
- Pinch of salt

DIRECTIONS

- In a deep bowl add in all the ingredients and toss to combine. To make the dressing, simply whisk all the ingredients together and drizzle over the salad and toss again to combine. Transfer to serving bowl and serve.

Flax Waffles

Whole grain brunch. Flax seed is a real super-food and a must for heart-healthy cooking.

Serving: 6

INGREDIENTS

- 2 eggs, beaten
- 177ml low fat milk
- 60ml canola oil
- 100g organic zucchini, grated
- 1 tsp vanilla extract
- 150g 100% stone ground whole wheat pastry flour
- 75g flax seed meal
- 50g oatmeal
- 40g all-purpose flour
- 4 tsp baking powder
- 1 tbsp sugar
- ¼ tsp salt

DIRECTIONS

- Using a food blender, blend the zucchini until smooth. In a mixing bowl, mix together all the wet ingredients, including the zucchini. In another bowl, combine the dry ingredients.
- Add the dry ingredients to the wet mixture and mix well to combine
- Cook your waffles in the desired size depending on your waffle iron and cook until lightly browned

Oatmeal Blueberry Cups

These muffins can also be made with raspberries

Servings: 5

INGREDIENTS

- 300g banana, mashed
- 100g uncooked whole grain oats
- 1 egg
- 1 tsp baking powder
- 1 tsp vanilla
- 60g fresh blueberries

DIRECTIONS

- Preheat the oven to 220 degree Celsius and prepare your muffin tins.
- Combine the banana, oats, egg, baking powder and vanilla and mix well to combine. Add in the berries. Scoop the mixture into the prepared muffin tins and bake for 6 mins then lower the oven temperature to 190 degree Celsius and bake for additional 12 mins.
- Cool muffins on wire rack and serve.

Whole-Wheat Strawberry Cake

This cake can be served with fresh homemade juice. Avocado adds a nutty flavor and helps more with heart health.

Servings: 4

INGREDIENTS

Topping:

- 4 tbsp avocado
- 50g organic brown sugar
- 150g 100% stone ground whole wheat flour
- 80g whole grain oats
- Pinch of nutmeg
- Pinch of cinnamon

Cake:

- 2 eggs
- 50g unsweetened coconut, shredded
- 80g low-fat plain Greek yogurt
- 100ml low-fat milk
- 50g organic brown sugar
- 2 tsp vanilla extract
- 150g 100% stone ground organic whole wheat flour
- 100g spelt flour
- 1 ¼ tsp cinnamon
- 2 tsp baking powder
- 200g of strawberries, halved

DIRECTIONS

- Preheat your oven to 177 degree Celsius and prepare a baking tin with parchment paper.
- For the topping combine all the ingredients an using your hands, blend the ingredients with your fingertips until it resembles fine crumbs. Cover with cling film and refrigerate while you prepare the cake.
- In a bowl beat the eggs, sugar and vanilla. Add in the oil, yoghurt and milk and whisk until combined.
- Add in the dry ingredients and mix with a wooden spoon and mix until just combined, do not over mix.
- Pour the batter into the baking tin and sprinkle the topping crumbs and top with the strawberries, giving them a slight push into the batter. Bake for 30-40 min. Insert toothpick if it comes out clean its ready. Cool on wire rack before cutting.

Quinoa Fruit Bowl

You can substitute the fruits as desired

Servings: 2

INGREDIENTS

- 170g uncooked quinoa
- 250g fresh strawberries, quartered
- 100g fresh blackberries
- 100g fresh blueberries
- 150g mango, cubed

Glaze:

- 60ml organic honey
- 2 tbsp fresh lemon juice
- 1 tbsp basil, chopped, to garnish

DIRECTIONS

- Rinse and cook your quinoa as per instructions on the package and allow it to cool down.
- In a bowl, combine the cooked quinoa with the rest of the ingredients and toss to combine.
- To make the glaze, whisk the ingredients (except the basil) and drizzle over the fruits and toss to combine.
- Transfer to serving bowl and top with some basil.

Blueberry Oat Bars

These bars can also be eaten as a snack

Servings: 4

INGREDIENTS

- 180g oatmeal
- 150g 100% stone ground organic whole wheat flour
- 90g organic brown sugar
- 5 tbsp avocado
- 1½ tsp baking soda
- ½ tsp salt
- 300g fresh blueberries
- 1 tbsp sugar
- 1 tbsp corn starch

DIRECTIONS

- Preheat your oven to 180 degree Celsius and prepare a baking sheet with parchment paper.
- In a bowl, mix together the dry ingredients. Add in the avocado and mix well until well incorporated. Using 2/3 of the oatmeal mix, press it firmly into the baking sheet.
- In a bowl, combine the berries, sugar and the starch and toss to combine. Pour the berry mixture into the baking sheet on top of the oatmeal crust.
- Sprinkle the remaining oatmeal mixture on top of the berries and bake into the preheated oven for 25 mins until golden brown. Allow it too cool before cutting and serving.

Almond Granola Cereal

This recipe can be served with low-fat yoghurt and fresh fruit

Servings: 2

INGREDIENTS

- 150g oats
- 60g crisp brown rice cereal
- ½ tbsp coconut oil
- 60ml unsweetened low-fat almond milk
- 60ml organic honey
- 3 tbsp almonds, grounded
- 3 tbsp unsweetened coconut, shredded
- 2 tbsp 80% cocoa dark chocolate shavings

DIRECTIONS

- Preheat your oven to 180° Celsius and prepare your baking sheet with parchment paper.
- In a bowl, mix together the oats and cereal. In another bowl, whisk together the oil, milk and honey. Drizzle the honey glaze over the cereal mixture, and mix with a spatula until well combined.
- Spread the cereal mixture into your baking sheet and bake for 50 mins, make sure you stir it every 15 mins, until golden. Allow it cool down before cutting it. Once it cools, sprinkle the coconut and chocolate.

Baked Lentil Pancakes

A lighter and nutritious substitute for your high-calorie brunch. See, pancakes don't always have to be sweet (and bad for you).

Servings: 2

INGREDIENTS

- 100g rolled oats
- 150g 100% stone ground whole wheat flour
- 2 tsp baking powder
- ½ tsp of salt
- 75g cooked lentils
- 1 tsp vanilla
- 2 tsp organic honey
- 1 egg
- 200ml low fat almond milk
- 2 tsp raw apple cider vinegar
- 1 tsp coconut oil

DIRECTIONS

- Preheat the oven to 180 degree Celsius and lightly spray a loaf baking tin with flax oil spray.
- In a bowl, whisk the milk and vinegar. Add the eggs, lentils, vanilla, honey and coconut oil and whisk to combine.
- In another bowl, mix together the dry ingredients. Add your dry ingredients to your lentils mixture and stir with a spatula until incorporated. Pour the mixture into the prepared baking tin and bake for 40 mins until a toothpick inserted comes out clean and dry. Allow the pancake to cool for 6 mins before cutting up.

Chocolate Coconut Cereal

A smarter alternative to sugar-loaded breakfast cereals

Servings: 1

INGREDIENTS

- 60ml coconut oil
- 1 tbsp flax oil
- 60ml organic honey
- 160g old fashioned oats, uncooked
- 30g unsweetened coconut, shredded
- 50g walnuts, roughly chopped
- 65g 70% cocoa dark chocolate, coarsely chopped

DIRECTIONS

- Preheat the oven to 150 degree Celsius, prepare a non-stick baking sheet.
- In a saucepan over medium heat, melt the coconut and flax oil with the honey. Once melted, transfer to a bowl and add in the oats, coconut and walnuts and toss to combine.
- Press mixture onto the baking sheet and bake for 35 mins until golden brown. Allow it to cool before scarping it. When ready to serve, add the chocolate. Can be stored in an airtight container at room temperature and it can be kept in the freezer for up to two months.

Raw Berry Parfait

Who said breakfast in a mason jar can't be both healthy and yummy?

Servings: 1

INGREDIENTS

- 85g unsalted almonds
- 90g unsalted walnuts
- 30g chia seeds
- 30g flax seeds
- 30g pumpkin seeds

Cashew Cream

- 90g unsalted cashews, soaked
- 75ml water
- 2 tsp agave
- ½ tsp vanilla extract
- ¼ tsp cinnamon, grounded
- Pinch of salt
- 50g fresh strawberries
- 50g fresh blackberries

DIRECTIONS

- In a food processor add all the seeds and blend together.
- To make the cashew cream, blend all the ingredients together, you can add some water to adjust the consistency. In a mason jar or simply a cereal bowl, add a layer of berries, top with cashew cream, nuts and add another layer of berries and repeat until you reach the desired layer.

Super Quinoa Bowl

A breakfast bowl that fills you up with nutrients

Servings: 2

INGREDIENTS

- 100g quinoa, uncooked
- 200ml water
- 118ml low fat coconut milk
- 2 dried dates, chopped
- 1 tsp cinnamon, grounded
- 1/8 tsp nutmeg, grounded
- 1/8 tsp cardamom, grounded
- 2 tbsp pumpkin seeds
- 1 tbsp unsweetened coconut, shredded
- 1 tbsp golden raisins
- ½ banana, sliced thinly
- A handful of Goji berries
- 1 tbsp chia seeds
- 1 tbsp coconut flakes

DIRECTIONS

- Rinse the quinoa well until clear water is visible and place in a saucepan over medium heat and add the water, milk and dried dates and bring to a boil.
- Once it starts to boil, lower the heat and allow it to simmer for 15 min until the quinoa becomes soft.
- Add in the spices and seeds, along with the shredded coconut and raisins. Cook for additional 6 mins. You may add some water to adjust the consistency.

- When the quinoa is cooked, transfer to serving bowl and top with some banana slices, Goji berries, chia and coconut flakes. You may add a teaspoon of honey for a natural sweetener.

Pumpkin Cookies

A breakfast on the-go or simply a healthy pick-up snack for your heart

Yield: 12 cookies

INGREDIENTS

- 60ml coconut oil, melted
- 60ml organic honey
- 80g rolled oats
- 80g quick cooking oats
- 80g dried cranberries
- 80g pumpkin seeds
- 50g ground flax seeds
- 1 tsp pumpkin pie spice
- ½ tsp salt
- 118ml organic pumpkin puree
- 2 eggs, lightly beaten

DIRECTIONS

- Preheat oven to 180 degrees Celsius and prepare a baking sheet with parchment paper.
- In a saucepan over medium heat, melt the coconut oil with the honey. Once melted remove from the heat.
- In a large mixing bowl add all the remaining ingredients and mix well with a wooden spoon until well combined.
- Drop one tablespoon of the batter onto the prepared baking sheet, leaving a bit of space between the cookies. Lightly press down the cookie to flatten it. Bake for 20 mins until the edges are golden brown. Allow the cookies to cool on a wire rack before serving.

Toasted Berry Oats

Serving: 2

INGREDIENTS

- 80g rolled oats
- 2 tbsp coconut oil
- 240ml low- fat coconut milk
- 1/8 tsp sea salt
- 70g fresh berries (any kind)
- 1 tsp black cardamom, grounded
- 2 tbsp chia seeds
- 5 dried dates, coarsely chopped
- 45g unsweetened coconut chips
- 1 tbsp organic honey
- ½ banana, sliced

DIRECTIONS

- In a saucepan over medium heat, toast the oats for a few minutes while stirring. Add the coconut oil and stir for another minute. Add in milk, salt, berries, cardamom, chia, half the dates, half the coconut chips and the honey.
- Stir while it cooks until the desired consistency is reached.
- Once it is ready, transfer to serving bowls and top with the remaining dates and chips along with some banana slices.

Flax Muffins

These muffins are packed with nutritious properties.

Serving: 4

INGREDIENTS

- 150g 100% stone ground whole wheat flour
- 100g buckwheat flour
- 50g flax seeds
- 2 tbsp organic arrowroot powder
- 2 tsp baking soda
- 1 tsp baking powder
- ½ tsp salt
- 1 tbsp cinnamon
- 170ml low-fat almond milk
- 60ml organic honey
- 1 tbsp apple cider vinegar
- 2 tsp vanilla extract
- 175g zucchini, grated
- 50g walnuts, roughly chopped

DIRECTIONS

- Preheat oven to 180 degrees Celsius and prepare a 12 cup muffin tin and lightly spray with flax oil.
- Mix together the dry ingredients with a wooden spoon.
- In a mixing bowl, whisk the almond milk, honey, vinegar and vanilla. Add the dry ingredients and slowly mix with a wooden spoon until just combined.
- Toss in the zucchini and walnuts and mix. Scoop the batter into the muffin tin and bake for 25 mins until a toothpick inserted comes out dry and clean. Allow muffins to dry before serving them.

Coconut Quinoa

This recipe can also be cooked with oatmeal instead of quinoa, if you're one of those people with a quinoa-phobia.

Serving: 2

INGREDIENTS

- 100g quinoa, rinsed, uncooked
- 240ml low-fat coconut milk
- 2 tsp vanilla extract
- 1tsp sugar
- ¼ tsp nutmeg, grounded
- ¼ tsp cinnamon, grounded
- Handful of mixed dried fruit, chopped
- Handful of mixed unsalted nuts, chopped

DIRECTIONS

- In a saucepan over medium heat combine all the ingredients together and cook for 20 mins until the quinoa is cooked through.
- Transfer to serving bowl and top with dried fruit and toasted nuts.

Blueberry Crisp

The ultimate comfort dish

Serving: 8

INGREDIENTS

- 80g rolled oats
- 100g walnuts, halved, chopped
- 80g organic almond meal
- 40g unsweetened coconut flakes
- ¼ tsp salt
- ¼ tsp cinnamon
- 60ml 2 tbsp olive oil
- 60ml raw organic honey
- 300g fresh blueberries

DIRECTIONS

- Preheat the oven to 180 degrees Celsius. Prepare a baking dish. Arrange the blueberries in the bottom.
- In a bowl, combine together the walnuts, oats, almonds, coconut, salt and cinnamon. Pour in the oil and honey and mix. Pour the mixture on top the arranged blueberries and bake for 25 mins until golden brown.

Pomegranate Quinoa

Can be eaten as a cereal too!

Serving: 2

INGREDIENTS

- 100g quinoa, uncooked
- 300ml unsweetened low-fat coconut milk
- 1/8 tsp cardamom, grounded
- 2 tbsp coconut sugar
- 1 small persimmon, cut into 1-inch cubes
- 4 tbsp pomegranate seeds
- 1 handful raw unsalted walnuts

DIRECTIONS

- In a saucepan over high heat, cook the quinoa in water and bring to a boil. Once it boils, lower the heat and allow it to simmer for 15 mins.
- In the same saucepan, mix the quinoa with the milk, cinnamon, cardamom and sugar and cook until creamy for 6 mins.
- Transfer to serving bowls and top with the persimmon and pomegranate seeds and toasted walnuts.

Heart Healthy Lunch Options

Tuna Avocado Sandwich

You can use salmon instead of tuna. I also suggest a spicy mustard.

Servings: 2

INGREDIENTS

- 42g albacore tuna
- 1/2 avocado, sliced
- 1/2 tbsp chives
- 1 lettuce, chopped
- 1 red onion, sliced
- 1 tomato, sliced
- 1 tbsp low-fat plain Greek yogurt
- 2 slices of 100% whole grain bread

DIRECTIONS

- In a bowl, mmix together the tuna, avocado, chives, yogurt. Spread mixture on the bread and top with the remaining ingredients.

Super Salad

A light and delicious detox salad

Serving: 6

INGREDIENTS

- 400g canned artichoke hearts, rinsed
- 100g cherries, pitted
- 425g canned chickpeas, rinsed
- 1 large bunch kale leaves
- 30g red onion, diced
- 60ml freshly squeezed organic lemon juice
- 100g Farro
- 1 tsp sea salt
- 1 tsp coconut oil
- 60ml olive oil
- 75g unsalted toasted walnuts, halved

DIRECTIONS

- In a saucepan over medium heat cook the farro with 350ml of water and a pinch of salt. Bring to boil and lower the heat and allow it to simmer uncovered for 25 mins until the farro is cooked and tender. Transfer to a bowl.
- In measuring cup, whisk the olive oil, coconut oil, lemon juice and sea salt and pour over the warm farro and toss to combine.
- Add the rest of the ingredients to the farro and give it another toss to combine.
- Transfer to serving dish and top with the walnuts.

Black Bean Patty

This recipe can be served alongside a green salad

Serving: 4-6

INGREDIENTS

- 1 red onion, chopped
- 1 clove garlic, crushed
- 1 tbsp olive oil
- 190g black beans, cooked, divided
- 1 ½ tsp cumin, grounded
- ½ tsp smoked paprika
- 1 tsp chili, grounded
- 1 tsp sea salt
- Pinch of black pepper (optional)
- 50g quick oats
- 130g fresh corn

DIRECTIONS

- Preheat your oven to 200 degree Celsius and line a baking sheet with parchment paper.
- In a pan over medium heat, add and olive oil and sauté the onion with the garlic. Add in 126g of the black beans along with the spices and stir for a few minutes.
- In a food processor, blend the oats then add the bean mixture and blend together then place in a bowl.
- Add the remaining beans to the blended mixture along with the corn and using your hands mash it up. You can add some oats to help shape the patties. Line your shaped patties on the prepared baking sheet and bake for 35 min, flipping once halfway through.

Edamame Power Bowl

This recipe is best served warm

Serving: 4

INGREDIENTS

- 1 large avocado, peeled
- 1 ginger root, about a 2m piece
- 1 shallot, chopped
- 3 tbsp organic lime juice
- 2 tsp apple cider vinegar
- 1 tsp organic honey
- 2 tsp olive oil
- 3 tbsp fresh basil, roughly chopped
- 440g chickpeas
- ½ tbsp olive oil
- ¼ tsp sea salt
- ¼ tsp cumin, grounded
- ⅛ tsp cayenne pepper, grounded
- ⅛ tsp ginger, grounded
- 70g unsalted cashews
- 280g edamame, shelled, cooked
- 2 apples, chopped
- Pinch of black pepper (optional)
- 1 tbsp fresh basil, chopped, to garnish

DIRECTIONS

- Using a handheld blender, blend together the avocado, ginger root, shallot, lime juice, vinegar, honey, olive oil and the basil. This will be the dressing.
- In a pan over high heat, toast the chickpeas for 6 min, while stirring. Add the olive oil then the spices and the

cashews and mix together. Remove from the heat when the cashews are lightly browned.

- In a bowl, add the cashew mixture along with the cooked edamame and the apples and with salt and pepper. Drizzle 3 tablespoons of the dressing and toss to combine. Transfer to serving plate and garnish with basil.

Farro Grape Salad

It's Italian and whole grain!

Serving: 10

INGREDIENTS

- 450g red grapes, seedless, halved
- Pinch of sea salt
- Pinch of black pepper (optional)
- 2 bunches Concord grapes
- 230g farro
- 2 tbsp fresh rosemary, coarsely chopped
- 60ml olive oil
- 1 big red onions, sliced into 1cm-thick rounds
- 1 tbsp sherry vinegar
- 300g mixed greens

DIRECTIONS

- Preheat oven to 120 degrees Celsius and on a baking sheet arrange the red grapes and season with ½ tsp salt and place the Concord grapes in the centre of the red grapes and bake them for about 1 hour and 25 min until the grapes have shrunk in size.
- In a saucepan over medium heat, add the farro, half the rosemary and 1 tsp of salt and pour some water until it covers it by 2 cm. Bring to a boil and then lower the heat and allow it to simmer for 26 mins then you can drain it and transfer to a bowl.
- In a pan over medium heat, cook the onions in 1 tablespoon of oil and add the rosemary and stir for 2 mins. Lower the heat and allow the onions to become golden. Add another tablespoon of oil and stir the onions until both sides are the same color. Pour in the vinegar and 2 more tablespoons of the oil.

- Pour the onions onto the farro and toss to combine. Adjust seasoning and add in the red grapes and let it rest for 20 mins.
- Transfer to serving platter add the greens and top with the Concord grapes.

Bulgur Soup

A grain-filled hearty soup. Bulgur is a common Middle-Eastern / Turkish ingredient. With a little effort you can find some at an international store.

Serving: 4

INGREDIENTS

- 2 tbsp extra-virgin olive oil
- 1 organic carrot, chopped
- 1 celery stalk, chopped
- 1 shallot, sliced
- 1.5 litres water
- 200g brown lentils, rinsed
- 75g bulgur wheat
- 3 tablespoons sherry vinegar
- Sea salt
- Black pepper

DIRECTIONS

- In a deep pot over medium heat, cook the carrot, celery and shallot in the olive oil and stir for about 6 min until tender. Pour in the water and add the lentils. When it boils, lower the heat and allow it to simmer, partially covered, for about 21 mins.
- Add in the bulgur and cook until it becomes tender and chewy. Drizzle with vinegar and adjust seasoning then transfer to serving platter and serve.

Roasted vegetables with Pumpkin Seeds

Pumpkin-seed super-powers await.

Serving: 5

INGREDIENTS

- 1 medium head garlic,
- 60ml extra virgin olive oil
- Pinch of sea salt
- Pinch of black pepper
- 1 bunch carrots, peeled
- 1 bunch beets, trimmed
- 1 bunch beet greens
- 1 tbsp organic lemon juice
- 3 tbsp extra virgin olive oil
- 50g pumpkin seeds, hulled

DIRECTIONS

- Preheat the oven to 180 degrees Celsius. Bring a large pot of water to a boil and drop in the carrots for 3 mins. Remove from the water and add in the beets repeating the process but allow the beets to boil for at least 8 mins. When you remove the beets, run some cold water on them to stop the cooking process and start removing the peel. Cut out a square piece of aluminum foil and place the garlic along with a teaspoon of olive oil and wrap it. Place in the oven for 15. Once you remove the wrap from the oven, increase the heat to 220 degrees Celsius.
- Chop the carrots and beets and arrange on a baking sheet and drizzle with 2 teaspoons of olive oil and sprinkle with sea salt. Bake into the preheated oven for 15 mins while flipping halfway through.

- On a baking sheet arrange the chard and beet greens and drizzle with 1 teaspoon of olive oil and a tiny pinch of sea salt and bake for 7 min.
- To make the dressing, peel the roasted garlic and mash it, add lemon juice and a small pinch of sea salt and olive oil and whisk to combine.
- Now you need to toast the pumpkin seeds, in a small pan over medium heat pour ½ tsp olive oil and toss the seeds, stirring until they start to pop, set aside to cool.
- In a bowl toss together the carrots and the beets and pour in the dressing. On a platter layer the roasted chard and top with the beets and carrots and drizzle the remaining dressing. Sprinkle with the toasted seeds and a pinch of black pepper.

Tofu Tacos

This recipe is great with some kale slaw. You'll live to 140 if you keep eating like this.

Serving: 8

INGREDIENTS

- 400g extra firm tofu, sliced into 8 equal slabs
- 3 tbsp low-sodium soy sauce
- 2 tbsp olive oil
- 2 tsp curry powder
- 1/2 of avocado, diced
- 8 whole wheat tortillas

Pintos:

- 1 tbsp olive oil
- 1 onion, sliced
- 4 cloves garlic, crushed
- 1 organic tomato, cubed
- ¼ tsp red pepper flakes
- ½ tsp salt
- 350g pinto beans, cooked
- 3 tbsp fresh cilantro, chopped

DIRECTIONS

- In a bowl, mix together the soy sauce, olive oil and curry.
- Spray a grill pan with flax oil spray and preheat. Coat each slab of tofu into the curry and grill for 8 mins on each side until grill marks appear on it. When you are ready to serve the tofu, slice the slabs into four strips lengthwise.

- In a pan over medium heat cook the onion and add a pinch of sea salt and sauté for 4 minutes. Add in the garlic then the tomato, red pepper and salt and cook for 4 more minutes. Add in the beans and cilantro and remove from the heat.
- Arrange the tacos, tofu and top with the beans.

Black Bean Dip

This recipe can be served with whole-wheat bread slices

Serving:4

INGREDIENTS

- 2 garlic cloves
- 1 ginger, a 2m piece
- 350g black kidney beans, rinsed
- Juice of ½ an organic lime
- 1 tbsp olive oil
- 1 tsp hemp oil

DIRECTIONS

- In a food processor blend all the ingredients together. Transfer to a bowl, drizzle a bit of olive oil on top and serve.

Bean Hummus

This recipe can also be served with grilled whole-wheat bread slices

Serving:4

INGREDIENTS

- 300g black beans
- 3 tbsp cilantro, chopped
- 1 clove garlic, minced
- 2 tbsp organic lime juice, freshly squeezed
- 1 tbsp tahini sauce
- 1 tsp coriander seed, grounded
- ½ tsp sea salt
- 60ml hemp oil

DIRECTIONS

- In a food processor blend all the ingredients together until it becomes into a thick paste consistency. Transfer to a bowl, drizzle a bit of olive oil on top and serve.

Mini Flax Bites

This recipe can be made in different sizes. Notice the heart-healthy power-combination of ingredients like hemp, almonds, etc as well as the flax.

Serving:4

INGREDIENTs

- One package of flax crackers
- 3 tbsp pesto sauce

Pine nut paste:

- 60g pine nuts
- 60g walnuts
- 2 tsp organic lemon juice, freshly squeezed
- 1/4 tsp salt
- 2 tsp yeast
- 60 ml water

Sauce

- 4 tomatoes, pitted, cubed
- 30g sun-dried tomatoes, soaked in olive oil
- 1 dried date
- 1 clove garlic
- 2 tsp hemp oil
- 1 tbsp fresh basil
- 1 tbsp dried oregano
- 2 tsp organic lemon juice, freshly squeezed

DIRECTIONS

- Arrange the crackers as a base.

- Blend all the pine nut paste ingredients in a food processor. Spread on top the cracker base.
- Next blend all the sauce ingredients. Spread on top the pine nut paste.
- Top with the pesto and garnish with some olives and a sprinkle of Italian dressing.

Burrito in a Bowl

Many healthy ingredients of a Cali-Mexican style mixed together.

Serving:4-6

INGREDIENTS

- 250g quinoa
- 3 tbsp flax seeds
- 400g grape tomatoes , halved
- 400g sweet corn
- 1 bell pepper, cubed
- 350g black beans, rinsed
- 1 red onion, cubed
- 1 bunch of cilantro, finely chopped
- 1 jalapeno, cubed
- Juice of 4 organic limes, freshly squeezed
- 1 large avocado, sliced
- Pinch of sea salt
- Pinch of black pepper (optional)

DIRECTIONS

- In deep pot over high heat, bring to a boil 1 litre of water and sprinkle a pinch of sea salt. Add in the quinoa, cover and cook for 15 mins. Once the quinoa is cooked, remove from the heat and place it aside covered.
- Mix the onion, lime juice and sea salt and add the remaining vegetables and toss to combine. Adjust seasoning.
- Sprinkle the flax seeds over the cooked quinoa, fluff it with a fork and mix, then add in the beans and the vegetables. Transfer to serving plates and top with avocado slices.

Tuna Avocado Sandwich

Many heart healthy oils jam-packed together.

Servings: 1

INGREDIENTS
- 42g albacore tuna
- ½ avocado, sliced
- ½ tbsp chives
- 1 lettuce, chopped
- 1 red onion, thinly sliced
- 1 tomato, sliced
- 1 tbsp low-fat plain Greek yogurt
- 2 slices of 100% stone ground whole grain bread

DIRECTIONS

- In a bowl, mix together the tuna, avocado, lettuce, chives and yogurt. Spread mixture on the bread and top with the onion and tomato slices.

Heart Healthy Dinner Options

Sweet Potato Quinoa

If you don't like quinoa, you don't have to pretend you like it just to make me happy. But I think it's a great food.

Servings:4-6

INGREDIENTS

- 150g quinoa, rinsed
- 350ml vegetable broth
- 1 tbsp extra-virgin olive oil
- 2 cloves garlic, crushed
- 1 small onion, diced
- 2 tsp fresh ginger root, diced
- 300g sweet potatoes, cubed
- 100g Brussel sprouts, sliced
- 2 tsp dried cranberries
- 30g unsalted almonds, sliced

DIRECTIONS

- In a pot, cook the quinoa as per instructions on the package.
- In a pan, heat the oil and add the onion and garlic and stir for 2 mins. Add the sprouts and sweet potato and cook until the potato becomes soft. Add in the quinoa and remove from the heat. Add in the cranberries and almonds, toss to combine. Serve warm.

Butternut Squash Bulgur

You can substitute the bulgur with quinoa. Then again, you can substitute anything with quinoa.

Serving:2-4

INGREDIENTS

- 1 small butternut squash , cubed
- 2 tbsp hemp oil
- 1 tsp sea salt
- 70g bulgur
- 240ml water
- ¼ tsp salt
- ½ bunch of parsley, chopped
- ½ bunch of mint, chopped
- 50g shallot, diced
- 50g dried cranberries, chopped
- Juice of 1 organic lemon, freshly squeezed
- 4 tsp olive oil

DIRECTIONS

- In a large pan over medium heat, cook the butternut in the hemp oil and add the salt. Stir and cover. Cook for 6 mins, uncover and allow it to cook for an additional 6 mins until the butternut is soft and golden on the edges. Transfer to serving plate.
- In a pot of water, over high heat, add the bulgur and bring it to a boil. Lower the heat and bring to a simmer for about 9 mins. Remove from the heat and place the pot aside, covered for6 mins. Fluff out the cooled bulgur using a fork and adjust seasoning. Place aside to cool completely.

- Add the bulgur to the serving plate that has the butternut and give it a quick toss to combine. Add in the parsley, mint, shallot and cranberries, giving it a gentle toss. Drizzle the lemon juice and olive oil on top and serve.

Pumpkin Soup

A perfect meal when served with a green salad

Serving:4

INGREDIENTS

- 450g organic 100% pumpkin puree
- 40g shallots, diced
- 3 cloves garlic, crushed
- 480ml vegetable broth
- 240 ml low-fat coconut milk
- 2 Tbsp organic honey
- Pinch of sea salt
- Pinch of black pepper
- ¼ tsp cinnamon
- ¼ tsp nutmeg

DIRECTIONS

- In a pot over medium heat. Add one tablespoon of olive oil and toss in the shallot and garlic and stir for 3 min. Add in the remaining ingredients for the soup and allow it to simmer.
- Remove from the heat and using a handheld blender, blend the soup until all the lumps are gone and it becomes smooth. Return to the heat and cook for 10 more mins and check seasoning. Serve warm.

Black Rice with Pumpkin

Serving:4

INGREDIENTS

- 240ml water
- 150g black rice, uncooked
- ¼ tsp salt.
- 1 small pumpkin, cubed
- 1 tbsp olive oil
- 1 clove garlic, crushed
- Pinch of salt
- 50g pumpkin seeds
- 1/2 tsp olive oil
- 1 tbsp cumin seeds
- 50g cilantro, chopped
- 56g goat cheese, crumbled
- Harissa, to garnish

DIRECTIONS

- Preheat your oven to 200 degrees Celsius.
- In a pot over medium heat cook the rice in the water adding a pinch of salt and bring to a boil, then lower the heat to minimum and allow the rice to simmer for about an hour. Place it aside to rest for 15 mins and then gently fluff it with a fork.
- In a bowl, mix together the pumpkin, olive oil and garlic and transfer to a baking sheet and sprinkle with some salt and bake until tender for about 15 mins.
- Mix the pumpkin seeds with olive oil and spread on a baking sheet and toast in the oven for about 5 mins.
- In a pan over medium heat, toast the cumin seeds and remove from the heat and crush them. Place them into the cooked rice and mix.

- Transfer the rice into the serving bowls and top with the pumpkin, the seeds, cilantro and goat cheese. You can also top with a little bit of Harissa.

Spinach Orzo Soup

Serving:4-6

INGREDIENTS

- 20ml extra-virgin olive oil
- 1 onion, diced
- 2 carrots, cubed
- 2 celery, chopped
- 3 cloves garlic, crushed
- 1.5 liters vegetable stock
- 400g fire-roasted tomatoes, diced
- 230g whole wheat orzo pasta
- 1/4 tsp dried oregano
- 1/4 tsp dried rosemary
- 900g spinach
- Salt
- Black pepper

DIRECTIONS

- In a pot over medium heat, add the oil with the onion and cook for 3 minutes until tender. Add in the carrots, celery and garlic, stirring for 3 minutes. Pour in the vegetable broth along with the rest of the ingredients, excluding the spinach. Bring to a boil, and lower the heat and allow it to simmer for 10 more minutes.
- Add in the spinach and cook for 2 mins until wilted. Adjust seasoning and serve warm.

Roasted Vegetables with Quinoa

Want to make a bunch of uptight people angry all at once? Then pronounce quinoa (keen-wah) as kwin-oh-a out-loud in a Whole Foods.

Serving: 8

INGREDIENTS

- 200g quinoa
- 280ml water
- ¼ tsp salt
- 450g butternut squash, cubed
- 400g Brussels sprouts, trimmed, halved
- 1 large red onions, chopped into large chunks
- ½ tsp dried thyme
- A dash of olive oil
- Sea salt
- Black pepper, freshly grounded

Dressing

- Juice of 1 organic lemon
- 1 clove of garlic, minced
- 1 tsp Dijon mustard
- ¼ tsp sugar
- ½ tsp sea salt
- Pinch of black pepper
- 70ml extra-virgin olive oil

DIRECTIONS

- Preheat the oven to 200 degree Celsius. Cook the quinoa as per instructions on the package.

- On a baking sheet, arrange the veggies and drizzle olive oil and toss to evenly coat, sprinkle with salt and pepper and scatter the thyme stems. Roast in the oven for half an hour making sure that you stir every 10 mins until cooked through. Remove the thyme stems.
- To make the dressing, simply whisk the lemon juice with garlic, mustard, sugar and of course salt and pepper until the sugar dissolves. Pour in the olive oil and whisk to combine.
- Once ready to serve, place the quinoa into the serving bowl and arrange half of the vegetables and then stir the quinoa with the vegetables. Arrange the remaining vegetables on top and drizzle with some of the dressing.

Pesto Pasta with Pepitas

Serving: 2

INGREDIENTS

- 1 large sweet potato
- 230g whole grain pasta, uncooked
- 3 heirloom tomatoes, sliced
- 2 tbsp pumpkin seeds

Pesto:

- 200g kale leaves
- 2 tbsp basil leaves
- 1 tbsp oregano leaves
- 3 garlic cloves
- 1 tbsp miso sauce
- 2 tbsp coconut oil
- 1 tbsp lemon juice
- Pinch of black pepper
- Pinch of sea salt
- 50g unsalted walnuts
- 3 tbsp nutritional yeast
- 1/2 avocado
- Water

DIRECTIONS

- Preheat the oven to 220 degrees Celsius. Prepare a baking sheet lined with foil. Poke the sweet potato and place on the baking sheet and roast for 30 minutes. Then flip it and roast for another 30 minutes. When it is cooked through, wrap it in foil and place it aside.
- Cook your pasta as per instructions on the package.

- Make the pesto by bending all its ingredients in a food processor until smooth, adding water and oil to adjust flavor and consistency. Mix the pesto with your pasta until evenly coated and place in serving bowl along with the potato and tomato slices and sprinkle with pepper and the pumpkin seeds.

Vegetable Bake with Rice

Serving:7

INGREDIENTS

- 675g whole grain rice
- 800ml water
- 1 tsp garlic powder
- 1 tsp paprika
- ¼ tsp sea salt
- 1 tbsp extra-virgin olive oil
- 1 small eggplant, cubed
- 2 small bell peppers, cubed
- ½ large onion, cubed
- 8 broccolini spears, cubed
- 2 small tomatoes, cubed
- 2 tsp olive oil
- 2 tbsp onion powder
- 1 tsp garlic powder
- 1 tsp paprika
- ¼ tbsp low-sodium soy sauce
- ½ tsp fennel seeds
- Pinch of sea salt
- Pinch of black pepper
- Pinch of red pepper flakes

DIRECTIONS

- Preheat oven to 176 degree Celsius and prepare a baking sheet. Arrange all the vegetables on the tray and drizzle with olive oil and sprinkle the spices. Toss to combine and roast for 26 mins until soft.
- Cook the rice in the water for 15 mins and bring to a boil. After 10 minute of boiling, lower the heat and allow it to

simmer for additional 30 mins until the rice is soft. Remove from the heat and add the garlic, paprika and the olive oil and mix.

- In a baking dish place the bake along with the rice and mix. Bake for an hour at a temperature of 148 degree Celsius. Serve warm.

Farro with Black Currants

Other nuts can be used in this recipe.

Serving: 2

INGREDIENTS

- 1 red onion, cubed
- Olive oil
- Sea salt
- 200g of semi-pearled farro
- 30g dried currants
- Dash of white balsamic vinegar
- 3 tbsp pine nuts
- A handful of mustard greens (any kind)

DIRECTIONS

- Preheat the oven to 220 degree Celsius. In a large pot, bring water to boil for the farro. Once it boils add the farro with one teaspoon of salt and cook for 15 minutes.
- On a baking sheet place the onions with a drizzle of olive oil and a sprinkle of salt and roast in the oven for 14 minutes until cooked through.
- Place currants in a small bowl. Moisten with 1 tablespoon boiling water and 1 tablespoon white balsamic vinegar. Set aside. Toast pine nuts in a small dry skillet over medium heat until golden brown — watch them carefully! Set aside.
- In a bowl, add the greens and the roasted onion along with the cooked and drained farro. Adjust seasoning and drizzle some olive oil plus vinegar and mix to combine. Add the currants and place farro into serving bowl and top with pine nuts.

Wild Rice and Fruit

A simple but gourmet cold mix of wild rice, fruits, and various exotic flavors.

Serving: 4

INGREDIENTS

- 275g wild rice, rinsed and drained
- 1 tbsp coconut oil
- 750ml vegetable broth
- 2 ripe nectarines, pitted, sliced
- 1 ripe peach, pitted, sliced
- 60g mint, chopped
- 1 small shallot, chopped
- 1 clove of garlic, crushed
- Juice of one large orange, freshly squeezed
- 2 tbsp olive oil
- 1 tbsp red wine vinegar
- Pinch of sea salt
- Almond slivers, to garnish

DIRECTIONS

- In a pot over medium heat, add the drained rice along with the coconut oil and stir. Add in the vegetables and pour in the broth, then lower the heat and allow it to simmer until the rice absorbs the liquid. Once cooked, remove from the heat and let it cool.
- For the dressing, in a bowl, combine together the shallot, garlic and orange juice. Drizzle the olive oil along with the vinegar and sprinkle a pinch of salt and mix to combine.
- In your serving bowl, mix the rice with the peaches, nectarine, mint and drizzle the dressing and place in the fridge for20 minutes. Once ready to serve, top your rice with a handful of chopped mint and a handful of almond.

Dessert (Heart Healthy Cookbook)

There's no reason to assume desserts should be skipped for your heart-healthy diet. In fact, these desserts are among the healthiest options in this cookbook.

Super Flax Bars

These bars can be stored up to one week in the fridge

Yield: 15 bars

INGREDIENTS

- 150g unsalted walnuts
- 50g chia seeds
- 50g ground flax seeds
- 50g hemp seeds
- 60g cacao nibs
- 50g coconut flakes
- 75g pumpkin seeds
- 70g raisins
- 100g dates

- 2 tbsp melted coconut oil

DIRECTIONS

- Blend all the ingredients together in a food processor. Press into a lined baking tin and allow it to set in the fridge for at least an hour. Cut the bars and serve cold.

Andrea's Dark Chocolate Pudding

There are some secrets hiding in this innocuous brown pudding. Almond milk, added texture from brown rice, and berries of choice (try acai for added health), lightly sweetened by just honey, makes this into a really special pudding.

Serving:4-6

INGREDIENTS

- 225g brown rice
- 3 cups unsweetened low-fat almond milk
- ½ tsp cinnamon
- 1 pinch of sea salt
- 60ml honey
- ¼ cup cocoa powder
- Berries, to garnish

DIRECTIONS

- In a saucepan over medium heat, add together rice, milk, cinnamon and salt and bring to a boil. Reduce the heat and let it simmer, covered and cook for an hour.
- Remove from the heat and add the honey and cocoa powder and adjust the consistency with almond milk. Serve warm with a handful of berries on top

Blueberry Frozen Yogurt

You can substitute the blueberries with raspberries or even acai berries that are among the healthiest.

Servings: 4

INGREDIENTS

- 400g fresh blueberries
- 200g low-fat Greek yogurt
- 90ml agave nectar
- ¼ tsp vanilla extract

DIRECTIONS

- Blend all the ingredients together in a food processor. Transfer to a freeze safe container and freeze it for four hours. You must stir it every hour. Serve cold.

Easy-to-Make Berry Tart

Serving: 6

INGREDIENTS

- 1 package whole wheat graham crackers
- 1 banana
- 1 tbsp Honey
- 170g low-fat Greek yogurt
- 118ml low-fat milk
- 5 ice cubes
- 1 tsp vanilla extract
- 2 tbsp unsweetened coconut, grated
- Berries, an assortment of colors—raspberries, blueberries, etc.

DIRECTIONS

- Preheat the oven to 200 degree Celsius.
- In a food processor blend the crackers with the banana. In a tart tin, spread out the dough to form the crust and spread the honey on top. Bake for 20 mins until lightly browned.
- Blend together the milk and the ice cubes then add the yogurt and vanilla and mix. Pour the yogurt mixture into the baked tart crust and top with the berries decoratively, and let it set in the fridge for at least an hour.

Secret Oatmeal Muffins Recipe

You can share this recipe with your friends, but then I'll have to kill you.

Yield: 12 muffins

INGREDIENTS

- 180g rolled oats
- 150g 100% stone ground whole wheat flour
- 3 tsp baking powder
- ½ tsp salt
- 1½ tsp cinnamon
- ½ tsp nutmeg
- 2 organic eggs
- 4 tbsp vegetable oil
- 60g sugar
- 130ml milk
- 2 ripe bananas, mashed
- 2 small apples, grated

DIRECTIONS

- Preheat your oven to 200 degree Celsius.
- In a bowl, mix the dry ingredients.
- Beat the sugar and eggs until light in color and add the oil then the milk.
- Add your dry ingredients and mix with a rubber spatula then add in the banana and apple.
- Scoop mixture into sprayed muffin tins and bake for 25 minutes until a toothpick inserted comes out dry and clean.

Blueberry Cobbler

Top this cobbler with a scoop of low-fat frozen yogurt.

Serving: 9

INGREDIENTS

- 400g blueberries
- ¼ tsp xanthan gum
- 2 tbsp sugar
- 1 tsp freshly squeezed organic lemon juice
- 2 tbsp avocado, melted
- 100g almond flour
- 2 tbsp honey
- ½ tsp organic lemon zest

DIRECTIONS

- Preheat the oven to 200 degree Celsius and prepare a baking dish.
- In a bowl, mix the berries with sugar and lemon juice. Pour into the baking dish. m
- Mix the avocado with the almond flour and lemon zest until it becomes a crumbly dough. Sprinkle the dough on top the blueberries and bake for 24 mins until golden. Serve cold or warm.

Banana Bake

This recipe is gluten and refined sugar free. Almond milk, oats, and your favorite brand of nutritious protein powder are all good for the ticker.

Serving: 4-6

INGREDIENTS

- 90g gluten free oats
- 60g protein powder
- 1 tsp baking powder
- 250g banana, mashed
- 1 tbsp vanilla extract
- 4 egg whites
- 240ml low-fat unsweetened almond milk

DIRECTIONS

- Preheat oven to 180 degree Celsius, prepare a baking tin.
- Add all the ingredients together in one bowl, leaving the egg whites last.
- Pour into the baking tin and bake for 35 minutes until cooked through. Cool before serving them

Cantaloupe Sorbet

You can use a variety of fruits for this recipe.

Serving: 4-6

INGREDIENTS

- 1 large ripe cantaloupe, chopped
- 60ml honey
- 2 tbsp organic lemon juice
- 2 tsp unflavored gelatin
- 80ml cold water
- 230g vanilla fat-free yogurt

DIRECTIONS

- In a food processor, blend the cantaloupe, honey and lemon juice. Transfer to a bowl and place aside.
- In a saucepan, sprinkle the gelatin over the cold water and let it stand for a minute then on low heat cook it, while stirring, until the gelatin dissolves. Then add in the cantaloupe mix and stir. Add the yogurt and stir again. Pour into a freeze safe container and freeze it until it becomes firm.
- Using a mixer, break the frozen sorbet and scoop into serving bowls. Serve immediately.

Lemony Berry Parfait

Everyone loves parfait. Who doesn't like parfait?

Servings: 4

INGREDIENTS

- 250g plain low-fat Greek yogurt
- 100g low-fat vanilla pudding
- 2 tbsp lemon curd
- 1/2 tsp pure vanilla extract
- 2 tbsp honey
- Zest of 1 organic lemon
- 1 tbsp freshly squeezed organic lemon juice
- 300g berries
- Fresh mint leaves, to garnish

DIRECTIONS

- In a bowl, mix together the yogurt, pudding, lemon juice, curd and extract.
- In another bowl, whisk the honey along with the lemon zest and juice. Add the berries and gently stir to evenly coat the berries.
- Assemble the parfait in serving glasses, scooping the yogurt in first then top with some berries and another layer of yogurt and more berries on top, garnish with fresh mint leaves.

Frozen Peanut Pie

A worthy final recipe for this collection. Have you made any of these recipes yet? Well put this silly booklet down and try to go make one if you haven't by now.

Serving: 10

INGREDIENTS

- 200g chocolate graham crackers, crushed into crumbs
- 7 tbsp sugar, divided
- 2 large egg whites, beaten
- 280ml low-fat milk
- 50g reduced-fat crunchy peanut butter
- 1/2 tsp vanilla
- 3 tbsp low-free cream cheese
- 230g low-fat Greek yogurt
- 60ml fat-free whip cream
- 3 tbsp roasted unsalted peanuts, roasted and chopped
- 70g dark chocolate, shaved

DIRECTIONS

- Preheat oven to 200 degree Celsius.
- Mix together the crumbs, 3 tablespoons of sugar and the egg whites. Press into the bottom of the pie tin as a crust. Bake for 10 mins.
- Mix the milk and remaining sugar in a saucepan over medium heat, remove from the heat and add the peanut butter and vanilla and whisk until combined. Cover and chill in the fridge for half an hour.
- In a bowl, beat the cheese with the yogurt and whip cream and milk and pour over the pie crust. Freeze it, uncovered, overnight until hard. The next day, top with dark chocolate shavings and the toasted peanuts. Sprinkle with peanuts and shaved chocolate. Serve cold.

Book Three: Andrea's Heart Healthy Smoothies

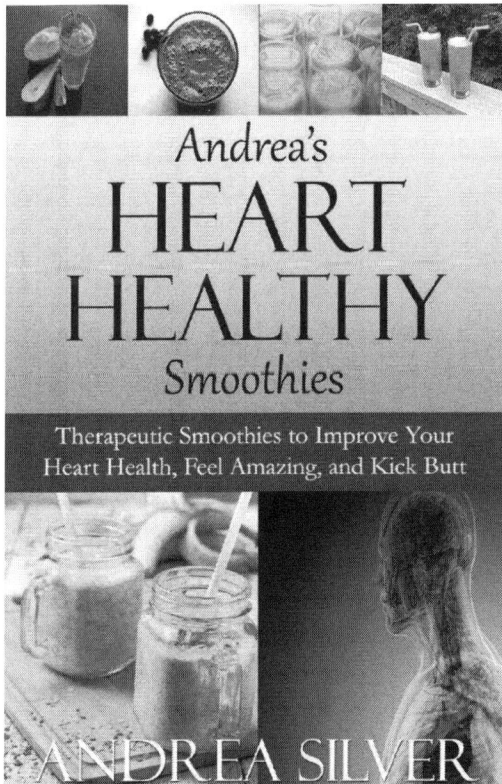

Andrea's HEART HEALTHY Smoothies

Therapeutic Smoothies to Improve Your Heart Health, Feel Amazing, and Kick Butt

ANDREA SILVER

Getting Started With Heart Healthy Smoothies

So, not long ago I created *Andrea's Heart Healthy Cookbook*, and I decided to do this follow-up. The reason is that I received a few e-mails from people that went something like this:

"Dear Andrea, I think all of your recipes are great. But, I don't have time to cook many of these fancier ones. I need to improve my diet, in particular for my heart, but I don't have the time or money to invest. Do you have any quicker recipes?"

So that's when I decided to create a heart-healthy strategy that can be taken care of by having one or two highly nutritious smoothies per day. The challenge was to find the right ingredients that would still do the job, in liquid form—and still taste really good.

The Basic Strategy

The first goal is to replace unhealthy fats with healthy, omega fatty acids. Some of the best sources include avocados and flax seeds. These are directly linked to heart health.

This should be combined with anti-inflammatory effects of polyphenols / flavinoids, like those found in ingredients like turmeric and green tea. Studies have shown that reducing inflammation is critical for the prevention of heart disease. That our regular diets are highly inflammatory by nature, and it's more important than ever to reduce this.

Next, we can improve overall organ health through the antioxidants in certain fruits and vegetables. Super-foods like kale are loaded with important vitamins, minerals, and antioxidants. Other seeds like pomegranate are excellent antioxidant sources, as well as berries (such as acai).

Bad Food Avoidance

Of course, a heart healthy diet is not possible if you counteract the recommendations above with foods that deliver the opposite effects.

It's important to avoid inflammatory foods. This includes simple carbs (white bread, cakes, etc). Further, sodas are not only very acidic (which is bad for organ health), but also inflammatory by nature—avoid them!

We know, of course, that bad fats—in particular trans fat (AKA partially hydrogenated oil) is a quick ticket to artery clogging. The same can be said for the fat produced by deep-frying just about anything in butter, or any fatty meat like bacon.

Excessive red meats, aside from increasing your cancer risk, also increase your risk of heart disease. These should be scrapped, too. If you're going to eat any meat along with your smoothies, start buying omega rich salmon.

Finally, take time to breath and relax! Stress is linked to coronary artery disease. The point of practices like yoga isn't just to be flexible and impress your friends by telling them you do yoga, but to learn to become grounded and focused into the moment, which can go a long way toward reducing daily stresses. I also suggest to take inventory of your life's problems and see how much you can start working out so you don't have to think about that nagging bill or responsibility that you put off anymore. Or if you're in a situation where your job is terrible—start thinking about a new career. These may be big changes, but I'm convinced no step is too big when it comes to improving your lifestyle / reducing stress, and therefore leading a longer life.

With all that being said, now let's tackle your smoothie recipes for optimal heart health.

,

Heart Healthy Smoothie Recipes

Avocado Banana Smoothie

Avocado / banana smoothies are very thick, so add more juice / water as necessary.

Servings: About 4

INGREDIENTS

- 236.59 ml orange-pineapple juice
- 1 banana, preferably very ripe & peeled
- 1 avocado, pitted & peeled
- 4 ice cubes

DIRECTIONS

- Mix everything together in a high speed blender and blend on high settings until light green & no ice chunks.

Classic Avocado Smoothie

Just pure avocado, enhanced a bit.

Servings: About 2

INGREDIENTS

- 1 avocado, preferably chilled & pit removed
- 177.44 ml cold milk
- 2 to 3 tbsp. sugar
- 1 tsp. lemon juice

DIRECTIONS

- Add everything together in a high speed blender and blend on high settings until smooth & no lumps are remaining.
- Taste and add more sugar if you feel you want it sweeter.

Vanilla and Cream Avocado Smoothie

Here's a rich variety of the classic avocado smoothie.

Servings: About 2

INGREDIENTS

- 1 avocado, large & scooped
- 1/2 tsp. vanilla essence
- 2 tbsp. caster sugar
- 118.29 ml cream
- 1 tsp. honey
- 473.18 ml milk

DIRECTIONS

- Put the avocado in a high speed blender and then add in the cream. Blend on high settings until smooth.
- Gradually add in the vanilla, milk, sugar & honey.
- Serve in glasses, large & chilled

Banana Avocado Flax Seed Smoothie

A double-serving of heart-healthy omega acids.

Servings: About 2

INGREDIENTS

- 1 banana, medium
- 1 avocado
- 709.77 ml milk
- 3 tbsp. sugar
- 100 g flax seeds

DIRECTIONS

- Mix everything together in a high speed blender in the sequence mentioned above and blend on high settings until you get your desired consistency.

Blueberry Banana Smoothie

Servings: About 1

INGREDIENTS

- 236.59 ml ice, crushed
- 1 banana, preferably peeled & in 3 to 4 pieces
- 118.29 ml fresh blueberries
- 1 tbsp. lime juice
- 78.07 ml coconut milk
- 1 tbsp. honey

DIRECTIONS

- In a high speed blender, add the banana first followed by the fresh blueberries, sugar, lime juice, crushed ice & milk.
- Blend until creamy and still smooth.

Creamy Blueberry Smoothie

Servings: About 2

INGREDIENTS

- 236.59 ml vanilla or plain yogurt
- 1 and 1/2 tbsp. honey
- 236.59 ml blueberries
- 177.44 ml ice cubes

DIRECTIONS

- Put everything together in a high speed blender & blend on high speed settings until smooth.

Orange & Blueberry Smoothie

Servings: About 1

INGREDIENTS

- 118.29 ml orange juice
- 200 grams blueberry yogurt, frozen & low fat
- 177.44 ml blueberries
- 70-80 ml pomegranate seeds

DIRECTIONS

- Put everything together (you may use frozen or fresh blueberries) in a high speed blender and blend on high settings until smooth. Taste and add a small quantity of sugar, if desired.

Green Tea & Blueberry Smoothie

Servings: About 2

INGREDIENTS

- 20 whole almonds, unsalted & dry-roasted; approximately 2 tbsp.
- 2 Matcha green tea bags
- 340.19 grams vanilla yogurt, non-fat
- 2 tbsp. flax seeds, ground
- 473.18 ml blueberries, frozen or fresh
- 3 ice cubes
- 177.44 ml water

DIRECTIONS

- To save time; you may brew the tea in advance. Add water in a large pan and heat until boiling. Once boiling, add in the tea bags; let them steep approximately five minutes.
- Squeeze & discard the tea bags.
- Allow the tea to chill for overnight.
- Place the blueberries in a freezer for overnight, if using fresh ones.
- Put blueberries together with the tea, yogurt, ice, flaxseed, and almonds in a high speed blender and blend on high until smooth.

Blueberry Apple Smoothie

Servings: About 2

INGREDIENTS

- 118.29 ml blueberries
- 236.59 ml vanilla yogurt
- 118.29 ml milk
- 236.59 ml apple, preferably peeled & chopped
- 4 to 5 ice cubes
- Sugar or splenda

DIRECTIONS

- Put everything together in a high speed blender & blend on high settings until smooth. Serve in a glass, preferably summery with a straw & garnish with a thin apple slice or fresh berry. Enjoy!

Turmeric and Berry Blend

This not-so-common combination is designed to give you an infusion of antioxidants and polyphenols. Turmeric the anti-inflammatory directly promotes heart health.

Servings: About 1

INGREDIENTS

- 236.59 ml blueberries
- 373.18 ml acai berries
- 236.59 ml milk
- 1 tbsp turmeric powder
- 1 tsp honey

DIRECTIONS

- Put everything in a blender & blend approximately a minute; then press the liquefy button until you get your desired consistency, approximately a minute more.
- Enjoy

Berries Magic

It's very magical. The most magical smoothie ever. There's no smoothie more magical than this one—I guarantee it.

Servings: About 2

INGREDIENTS

- 236.59 ml each blueberries, raspberries, & acai berries, frozen or fresh
- 118.29 ml vanilla yogurt, non-fat
- 236.59 ml unsweetened pineapple juice

DIRECTIONS

- To give your smoothie some chilly frost; don't forget to freeze some of the berries for some time and then place them all with pineapple juice and yogurt in a high speed blender. Blend on high settings until smooth.
- Pour into two large glasses & enjoy!

Lemon Blueberry Smoothie

A good source of ascorbic acid.

Servings: About 4

INGREDIENTS

- 236.59 ml blueberries, frozen or fresh
- 354.88 ml milk, nonfat
- 226.79 grams vanilla yogurt, smooth, creamy and low-fat (approximately 1container)
- 1 and 1/2 tsp. Crystal Light lemonade mix, low calorie & sugar free
- 236.59 ml ice cube

DIRECTIONS

- Place blueberries together with the yogurt, milk, & ice cubes in a high speed blender container; cover & blend on high settings until smooth. Transfer the mixture to large serving glasses & serve immediately.

Black & Blueberry Smoothie

Servings: About 3

INGREDIENTS

- 354.88 ml vanilla yogurt, frozen
- 78.07 ml each orange & cranberry juice
- 2 ice cubes
- 295.73 ml blueberries
- 1/16 tsp ground nutmeg
- 236.59 ml blackberries
- 100 ml flax seeds
- 2 tbsp. honey

DIRECTIONS

- Put everything together in a high speed blender and blend on high speed settings until smooth, approximately a minute. Pour the mixture into tall glasses & serve immediately.

Mango & Berry Delight

Has a bit of a nutty flavor with the almonds.

Servings: About 2

INGREDIENTS

- 236.59 ml orange juice
- 118.29 ml vanilla yogurt, frozen & non-fat
- 60 ml almonds
- 236.59 ml each blueberries, mango & strawberry, diced

DIRECTIONS

- Place everything together in a high speed blender's container; cover & blend on high speed settings until smooth. Transfer the mixture into two tall glasses & serve immediately.

Honey Banana Blueberry Turmeric Smoothie

It's a mouthful to say, I admit.

Servings: About 1

INGREDIENTS

- 1 large banana, broken into pieces
- 236.59 ml milk, low-fat
- 60 grams blueberries
- 1/2 tbsp. honey, raw or creamed
- 2 tsp turmeric powder

DIRECTIONS

- Add blueberries, banana & a cup of milk to your high speed blender or mixer.
- Blend well on high settings; until a nice lavender color forms. Add some fiber powder of your choice, the turmeric, and honey. Blend again until the honey has completely dispersed through the mix. Transfer to large serving glass and enjoy!

Kiwi Blueberry Smoothie

Servings: About 1

INGREDIENTS

- 158.51 ml blueberries, frozen or fresh
- 1 frozen banana, large
- 2 kiwi fruits, ripe & peeled
- 3 honey dates, (If using medjool then use one or two more)

DIRECTIONS

- Let the dates to soak in boiling or hot water approximately 5 to 10 minutes in a small bowl until soft.
- Remove the dates from water and transfer with other ingredients to a high speed blender; reserving a few of the blueberries for garnish, if desired. Blend on high settings until smooth. Add in the reserved berries; stir.
- Enjoy!

Blueberry Flax Seeds Smoothie

A heart-healthy power-blend that includes almond, avocado, and flax.

Servings: About 2

INGREDIENTS

- 1/2 avocado
- 118.29 ml blueberries, frozen
- 59.14 ml orange juice
- 118.29 ml soymilk, nondairy
- 2 tbsp. almond butter
- 78.07 ml strawberries, frozen
- 2 tsp. flax seeds, freshly ground
- 1 frozen banana, medium

DIRECTIONS

- Put everything together in a high speed blender and blend on high settings until smooth; stirring frequently.
- You may add more of frozen or liquid ingredients to your smoothie; if you want it to be thickened or thin.
- ENJOY

Totally Green Smoothie

Servings: About 1

INGREDIENTS

- 236.59 ml blueberries
- 141.74 grams spinach, fresh
- 1 tbsp. flax seed
- 118.29 ml pineapple
- 1 banana, medium and into pieces
- 236.59 ml soymilk, unsweetened

DIRECTIONS

- Combine everything together in a high speed blender & blend on high settings approximately a minute or so, until you get your desired consistency.

Pomegranate Smoothie

Servings: About 2

INGREDIENTS

- 1 banana, medium & peeled
- Pomegranate seeds
- 473.18 ml vanilla yogurt, non-fat
- 1 tbsp. coarse sugar
- 236.59 ml pomegranate juice

DIRECTIONS

- Using plastic wrap; wrap the peeled banana & let it freeze until frozen, approximately three hours or a little more.
- Unwrap the banana; breaking into small chunks and then put it in a blender with the juice & yogurt. Cover; blend until smooth; transfer the mixture into two large glasses to serve. If desired, you may top it with the pomegranate seeds.

Green Mango Smoothie

Spinach with mangos... it's a better tasting combo than you think!

Servings: About 1

INGREDIENTS

- 473.18 ml spinach
- 2 mangoes, ripe, peeled & diced
- 236.59 to 473.18 ml coconut water or plain water

DIRECTIONS

- Place everything together in a high speed blender & pulse on high settings until smooth. Add more of coconut water or water to get your desired consistency. Transfer to a large glass & serve!

Kale, Spinach, Flax Seeds & Orange Smoothie

OK, if this doesn't get you healthy, I don't know what will!

Servings: About 5

INGREDIENTS

- 1 tbsp. flax seeds, ground
- Mint, fresh & chopped
- 80 grams spinach
- 1 lemon
- 1/4 whole watermelon
- 3 oranges, large
- 150 grams kale
- 2 tbsp. coconut oil

DIRECTIONS

- Add spinach & kale in boiling water and let them steam approximately five minutes. After five minutes; let them cool at room temperature.
- Chop up everything.
- Add the fruit with water in a high speed blender & blend.
- Add the leftover ingredients & blend again until you get your desired consistency.

Banana Berry Green Smoothie

Servings: About 2

INGREDIENTS

- 2 bananas, medium & frozen or fresh
- 200 ml powdered hemp or hemp seeds
- 236.59 ml each blueberries & raspberries, frozen or fresh
- 473.18 ml each fresh spinach & unsweetened almond milk

DIRECTIONS

- To avoid leafy chunks; we suggest you to first blend the leafy greens & liquid together.
- Add the leftover ingredients, once it's nice & creamy and blend again. Enjoy!

Vanilla Blueberry Graham Protein Smoothie

Servings: About 2

INGREDIENTS

- 1 handful spinach
- 2 dates, preferably medjool pitted & chopped
- 1 medium banana, frozen
- 177.44 ml blueberries
- 1 tbsp. tahini or almond butter
- 2 tbsp. hemp seeds
- 1 tbsp. flax seed
- 236.59 ml coconut water
- 1 tbsp. oats
- 2 tbsp. graham crackers
- 1 scoop protein powder, vanilla

DIRECTIONS

- Put everything together in a high speed blender & blend on high settings until creamy & smooth.
- Check the liquid & adjust as per your desired consistency. Add more of liquid; if you like your smoothie a little runnier or add a few ice cubes; if you like your smoothie a little thicker.
- Sprinkle with graham crackers, preferably crushed & enjoy.

Avocado Chia Seeds Smoothie

Servings: About 2

INGREDIENTS

- 1 avocado, halved & pitted
- 4 whole ice cubes
- 1 tbsp. honey and more, if required
- 177.44 ml milk, low-fat
- 1 tbsp. chia seeds

DIRECTIONS

- Add milk, 1 cup of water, honey, avocados & ice cubes into your high speed blender; blend on high speed settings until smooth.
- If required; you may add more of honey. Add in the chia seeds; stir well & then pour into large glasses & immediately serve.

Blueberry Banana Chia Seeds Smoothie

Servings: About 2

INGREDIENTS

- 8 blueberries, frozen
- 236.59 ml yogurt, whole milk
- 118.29 ml banana, frozen
- 1 tbsp. chia seeds

DIRECTIONS

- Add everything together in a high speed blender and blend on high settings until smooth & creamy. Transfer the mixture to large glasses and serve.

Totally Red Smoothie

This is the reddest smoothie you'll drink. It's otherwise a great blend of antioxidants, omega fatty acids, etc. Maybe the healthiest smoothie in the book.

Servings: About 4

INGREDIENTS

- 1 beet, medium & fresh (170.09 grams)
- 1 banana, frozen or fresh
- 2 tbsp. flax seeds, ground
- 1 apple, medium & fresh (170.09 grams)
- 1 tbsp. ginger, fresh & grated
- Juice of 1 lime
- 1 carrot, medium & fresh (113.39 grams)
- 1 tbsp. chia seeds
- 907.18 grams water
- 1 tbsp. hemp seeds

DIRECTIONS

- Place everything together into the container of your high speed blender & process until smooth. Let the mixture to refrigerate for couple of hours and then serve.

Berry Chia Smoothie

Servings: About 2

INGREDIENTS

- 236.59 ml mango or guava juice
- 354.88 ml blueberries, frozen
- 1 banana, medium and cut into pieces
- 170.09 grams plain or vanilla yogurt
- 2 tsp. chia seeds
- Some Stevia

DIRECTIONS

- Place everything together (except the chia seeds) in a container of high speed blender & process until smooth. Add in the chia seeds; stir.

Chia Fruit Smoothie

Servings: About 2

INGREDIENTS

- 118.29 ml each blueberries & blackberries
- 14.17 grams chia seeds
- 1 banana, medium
- 1/2 peeled lemon
- 56.69 grams almond milk
- 1 scoop protein powder. I use rice or soy. Whey tastes better, but it gives you gas (sorry for being explicit, if you're going to buy a cheap cookbook on Amazon, it should at least be an honest one.)

DIRECTIONS

- Put protein powder and almond milk together in a high speed blender & liquefy. Add in the banana, lemon and berries; blend on high settings. Add in the chia seeds in the last & blend again.
- Set the mixture to freeze for a minimum period of 15 minutes or refrigerate for overnight.

Avocado Mango Honey Almond Smoothie

Yes, it's another mouthful to pronounce, but what you're getting is a nutty smoothie with an abundance of omega fatty acids to directly assist your heart health.

Servings: About 3

INGREDIENTS

- 480 ml mango nectar
- 150 ml crushed almonds
- 2 avocados, flesh scooped out
- 1/2 tsp. honey
- 8 to 10 ice cubes

DIRECTIONS

- Add the scooped avocado and almonds to the blender followed by the ice cubes and mango nectar.
- Blend on high settings. Stop; add in the honey and blend again.
- Serve & enjoy.

Berry Banana Dairy Smoothie

Servings: About 2

INGREDIENTS

- 118.29 ml blueberry yogurt, fat-free
- 236.59 ml blueberries
- 118.29 ml 2% milk
- 1 banana, large & frozen
- 236.59 ml strawberry, diced
- 118.29 ml cranberry juice

DIRECTIONS

- Put everything in your fabulous high speed blender and blend on high settings until smooth & creamy.
- Transfer into two large glasses & enjoy!

Blueberry Delight

Servings: About 4

INGREDIENTS

- 236.59 ml blueberries
- 1 banana, ripe
- 6 ice cubes
- 1 tsp. honey or Splenda
- 236.59 ml skim milk or orange juice

DIRECTIONS

- Put everything in the container of a high speed blender and blend on high settings until you get your desired consistency.
- Add more juice, if desired.

Hemp Supreme

Hemp is a key ingredient for heart health. Combined with wheat grass and you have a very healthy smoothie.

Servings: About 2

INGREDIENTS

- 226.79 grams water
- 1 banana, medium & ripe
- 2 scoops each protein powder & hemp seeds. You can also use hemp protein powder.
- 1 dash vanilla
- 118.29 ml blueberries, frozen
- 1 tbsp. wheat grass, powdered

DIRECTIONS

- Put everything together in a high speed blender and blend on high settings until smooth.

Flax & Blueberry Milkshake

Flax is infused with a large amount of omega fatty acids and many other nutrients. You can't miss adding flax to your smoothies!

Servings: About 1

INGREDIENTS

- 158.51 ml blueberries
- 4 packets stevia (1 gram)
- 1/2 tsp. cinnamon
- 3 tbsp. flax seed meal, freshly ground
- 1 tbsp. gelatin, unflavored
- 2 tbsp. raw sunflower seeds, freshly ground
- 236.59 ml skim milk
- 2 tsp. vanilla

DIRECTIONS

- Put everything together in a high speed blender and blend on high settings until smooth. Serve cold.

Blueberry & Peach Smoothie

Servings: About 1

INGREDIENTS

- 59.14 to 118.29 ml soy or rice milk.
- 1/2 peach, chopped
- 59.14 ml vanilla soy or rice ice cream
- 59.14 ml blueberries, frozen or fresh

DIRECTIONS

- Put everything together in a high speed blender and blend on high settings until smooth. Transfer into a large glass; enjoy!

Kale Blueberry & Spinach Smoothie

Yes, you can put kale in smoothies.

Servings: About 1

INGREDIENTS

- 236.59 ml spinach
- 236.59 ml orange juice
- 236.59 ml kale
- 236.59 ml berries, frozen
- Honey or Stevia to taste

DIRECTIONS

- Put everything together in a high speed blender and blend on high settings until smooth. Taste & add in more of the honey if desired and then transfer into a large glass; enjoy!

Kale Berry Fiesta

This elaborate smoothie fulfills many nutritious elements in one go.

Servings: About 1

INGREDIENTS

- 236.59 ml mixed berries such as acai or raspberries
- 1 beet, cooked
- 236.59 ml shredded kale
- 1 tbsp. maple syrup
- 236.59 ml coconut water
- 1 scoop protein powder, vanilla

DIRECTIONS

- Put everything together in a high speed blender and blend on high settings until smooth.

Blueberry Spinach/Kale Smoothie

Servings: About 1

INGREDIENTS

- 236.59 ml spinach or kale
- 473.18 ml ice
- 113.39 grams milk or water
- 1 scoop whey protein
- 236.59 ml blueberries, fresh or frozen
- 118.29 ml yogurt, plain

DIRECTIONS

- Add everything (except the protein) in a high speed blender; blend on high settings.
- Add in the whey protein & blend again, preferably on lower speed setting now.
- Serve & enjoy!

Green Pear Smoothie

Servings: About 2

INGREDIENTS

- 85.04 grams spinach
- 1 Bartlett pear, medium
- 2 bananas, medium & frozen
- 56.69 grams kale
- 1 tbsp. flax seeds, ground
- 118.29 ml almond milk
- Water
- Ice cube

DIRECTIONS

- Put everything together in a high speed blender and blend on high settings until smooth. Depending upon your likings; you may add ice cubes to make the smoothie thicker or water to make the smoothie thin.

Avocado Chocolate Smoothie

Avocado and chocolate is a surprisingly good combination. Nutty and full of flavor. Cocoa powder is also quite healthy. Combined with some spinach and this is great for your body and a power-house of heart healthy compounds.

Servings: About 2

INGREDIENTS

- 1 banana
- 354.88 ml spinach
- 1 avocado
- 118.29 ml water
- 3 tbsp. cocoa powder
- 236.59 ml almond milk
- 1 tbsp. chia seeds

DIRECTIONS

- Put spinach together with the almond milk, avocado & water in your high speed blender and blend on high settings until smooth.
- Add in the leftover ingredients & blend again until smooth.

Avocado Blueberry Chia Smoothie

Chia seeds are very good for your heart, combined with avocado's heart-healthy properties, and the antioxidants of blueberries.

Servings: About 1

INGREDIENTS

- 1∕8 avocado
- 59.14 ml plain yogurt
- 118.29 ml Blueberry, frozen
- 59.14 ml chia seeds, gel
- 1 tsp. honey, raw
- 236.59 ml Matcha green tea
- 1 dash vanilla

DIRECTIONS

- Place all of the ingredients together in a high speed blender (except tea & honey). Start chopping; add in enough tea and ensure that the ingredients blend well, and you get your desired consistency. Add honey and then blend on high settings until smooth & uniform. Transfer the mixture to a large glass with a straw and enjoy!

Tempting Berry Granola Blend

Servings: About 3

INGREDIENTS

- 236.59 ml ice cubes
- 354.88 ml strawberries, frozen
- 59.14 ml blueberries
- 177.44 ml orange juice
- 170.09 g blueberry yogurt
- 200 g granola

DIRECTIONS

- Put everything together minus the granola into a blender & blend approximately 10 to 20 seconds, until no ice chunks are remaining.
- Transfer the mixture into large glasses and garnish with the granola on top.

Strawberry & Blueberry Smoothie

Servings: About 1

INGREDIENTS

- 170.09 grams vanilla yogurt, non-fat
- 118.29 ml regular milk or vanilla soymilk
- 236.59 ml strawberry, frozen or fresh
- 118.29 ml blueberries, frozen or fresh

DIRECTIONS

- Put everything together in a high speed blender and blend on high settings until smooth.

Cereal & Protein Smoothie

Servings: About 2

INGREDIENTS

- 118.29 ml blueberries
- 2 tsp. whey protein powder
- 236.59 ml milk
- 1 tbsp. honey
- 118.29 ml all bran extra fiber cereal
- 6 ice cubes

DIRECTIONS

- Put everything together in a high speed blender and blend on high settings until smooth.

Blue & Red Smoothie

Servings: About 2

INGREDIENTS

- 236.59 ml strawberries, frozen & sliced
- 236.59 ml 2% milk, low-fat
- 236.59 ml blueberries, frozen
- 236.59 ml vanilla yogurt
- 200 g high fiber cereal or a fiber supplement
- 78.07 ml honey
- Whipped topping of choice
- Strawberry & blueberries to garnish

DIRECTIONS

- Put everything together (except whipped topping and garnish ingredients) in a high speed blender.
- Blend on high settings until smooth & creamy.
- Pour into large glasses & add topping. Garnish with berries.

Berries Combo Smoothie

Servings: About 4

INGREDIENTS

- 473.18 ml each blackberries & blueberries
- 1 tsp. vanilla extract
- 236.59 ml milk
- 473.18 ml yogurt, raspberry
- 2 tbsp. sugar
- 100 grams, or about ½ cup of high fiber granola
- 100 grams crushed almonds
- 473.18 ml ice

DIRECTIONS

- Place everything in a high speed blender. Cover & blend on high settings until smooth.
- Serve immediately.

Fruit Yogurt and Flax

Servings: About 2

INGREDIENTS

- 1 banana, small & into pieces
- 118.29 ml strawberry
- 236.59 ml apple juice
- 118.29 ml blueberries
- 236.59 ml yogurt, vanilla
- 230 g flax seed
- 473.18 ml ice

DIRECTIONS

- Place everything in a high speed blender. Cover & blend on high settings until smooth.
- Serve immediately.

Blueberry Yogurt Hemp Smoothie

No, hemp won't affect your urine tests. It's one of the healthiest ingredients for your heart.

Servings: About 2

INGREDIENTS

- 236.59 ml blueberries, frozen
- 1 to 2 tsp. sugar
- 236.59 ml yogurt, plain
- 75 ml hemp protein powder
- 50 g hemp seeds
- Milk, honey & ice

DIRECTIONS

- Place everything in a high speed blender. Cover & blend on high settings until smooth.
- Taste for sweetness & if required, you may add more of honey. Serve immediately.

Coconut Blueberry Smoothie

Servings: About 1

INGREDIENTS

- 118.29 ml coconut milk
- 158.51 ml blueberries, frozen
- 1/4 tsp. cinnamon
- 1 tbsp. honey

DIRECTIONS

- Place everything in a high speed blender. Cover & blend on high settings until smooth and blueberries are incorporated. Transfer the mixture, pour to a large glass & enjoy!

Watermelon Seed Blend Smoothie

A smorgasboard of all the healthiest seeds found so far in this book, with a tasty base.

Servings: About 4

INGREDIENTS

- 236.59 ml milk
- 236.59 ml blueberries, frozen
- 1 banana cut in pieces
- 150 g chia seeds
- 150 g flax seeds
- 100 g hemp seeds
- 236.59 ml watermelon

DIRECTIONS

- Place everything in a high speed blender. Cover & blend on high settings until smooth

Blueberry Nut Infusion

We conclude this recipe collection with a triple-combination of nuts, mixed with blueberries, that makes for an original flavor, with plenty of important fatty acids.

Servings: About 6

INGREDIENTS

- 473.18 ml blueberries, frozen
- 2 bananas, medium
- 473.18 ml skim milk
- 1 tbsp. honey or to taste
- 60 g crushed walnuts
- 60 g crushed almonds
- 60 g crushed cashews
- 473.18 ml vanilla yogurt, nonfat

DIRECTIONS

- Place everything in a high speed blender. Cover & blend on high settings until smooth.

Book Four: Andrea's Immune Boosting Smoothies

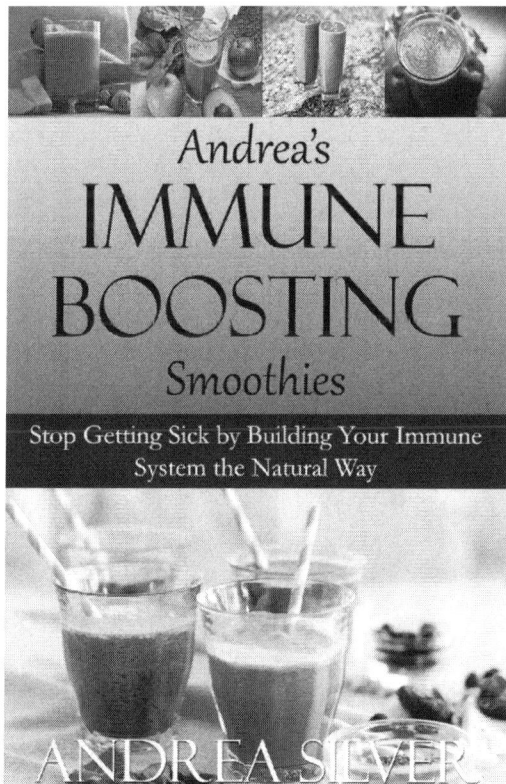

Getting Started With Immune Smoothies

There's always been something magical about those people with impenetrable immune systems. You know the ones—when you have that mysterious uncle who, despite being in a house full of flu germs, somehow just never gets sick.

They may have some dubious explanation behind their talent, like "Oh, I take vitamin C tablets". However, you know they're full of it. You take vitamin C tablets, too, and still you find yourself bed-ridden after coming within 30 feet of a kid coughing at the supermarket.

The truth is that such people have optimized immune systems. Viruses may enter their bodies, but they are immediately destroyed by a body operating at a high level of efficiency.

Your immune system has never been so important before. Given we're now in an age of "superbugs"—or antibiotic resistant bacteria—it's now more important than ever to try to become like that impervious uncle of yours who never gets sick.

But how can we do this? A big factor is your diet, another factor are your habits, and another factor are supplements. We'll go over each one briefly, so that you can get the most out of this book.

Your Dietary Habits

This is where this book comes in. Your diet should include plenty of ascorbic acid (vitamin C) in the form of various types of fruits. Some of the best sources are actually papaya, kiwis, and even tomatoes—all of which are included in these super-smoothies. Ascorbic acid is actually used by your body to break down the nucleic acid of viruses. It is also an antioxidant that promotes organ health, preventing oxidization of the organs and allowing them to function better.

Another important part of your diet is ginger, and it's why I suggest to have an ample supply of it from a health food store that you can add to your smoothies. Ginger has numerous important health effects, including improving your circulatory system, cleansing effects on the colon, reducing inflammation, and it also contains natural antibacterial, anti-viral chemicals.

Flavonoids, or plant metabolites, found in plenty of green "things" is also very important for your immune system, which is why you'll find many smoothies with important green booster plants, including kale and spinach.

For this book, I suggest drinking two such smoothies per day during the periods when you seek to strengthen your immune system.

Your Fidgeting Habits

It's also important to note that the way most people get sick is when fingers come into contact with mucous membranes. Although some habits are tough to break, a key to maintaining a healthy and virus-free body includes avoiding the following:

- Nose picking
- Eye rubbing
- Mouth rubbing
- Face rubbing,
- Doorknob licking

(I made the last one up.)

Many of us do these habits unconsciously, but they're unfortunately a quick ticket to getting sick. The sooner you can break these habits, the better off you'll be.

Your Supplements

A supplement is a specific ingredient that you take daily for medicinal purposes. Many vitamin pills on the market are questionable in my opinion. Instead, I prefer to buy my own ingredients, whether that involves powdering my own ginger / ginseng, or adding turmeric powder into my own capsules.

However, there is one particular supplement you can start taking for almost **guaranteed** results—garlic. This magic ingredient works to reduce infection by colds by 60% according to a study performed in the United Kingdom.

Some take garlic capsules, but I'm not crazy about this, and it's also unnecessarily expensive. Instead, do this: buy whole cloves of garlic, and eat the garlic bulbs **raw** every day—about 3-4 bulbs daily. Do this during cold and flu season, and it may just be the magic pill you're looking for. If you combine this technique with consuming 1-3 of the smoothies listed in this book per day, then you'll become a superhero.

(You can also check Amazon for my specialty garlic cookbook that I have out.)

* * *

With all of that being said, let's now turn to the smoothie recipes you've been waiting for. Enjoy!

Immune Smoothie Recipes

Carrot & Ginger Smoothie

A one-two punch of two famous immune boosting ingredients.

Servings: About 2

INGREDIENTS

- 4 carrots, unpeeled
- 1 celery stalk, with leaves
- 28.34 grams ginger, preferably thumb size piece & peeled
- 1 apple, unpeeled, cored & quartered

DIRECTIONS

- Put everything together, preferably in the order mentioned above in a juicer and process on high settings for a minute.
- Serve immediately & enjoy.

Tropical Berries Smoothie

Servings: About 2

INGREDIENTS

- 1 kiwi, peeled
- 473.18 ml blackberries, frozen
- 118.29 ml yogurt, plain & low-fat
- 236.59 ml banana, sliced
- 118.29 ml apple juice
- 236.59 ml red raspberries, frozen

DIRECTIONS

- Add everything together in a high speed blender & blend on high settings until smooth.

Strawberry Kiwi Smoothie

Servings: About 2

INGREDIENTS

- 6 strawberries, hulled & coarsely chopped
- 118.29 ml each pineapple & orange juice
- 1/2 banana, partially frozen
- 118.29 ml vanilla yogurt, frozen
- 1 kiwi, peeled & coarsely chopped

DIRECTIONS

- Place everything together in a high speed blender and blend on high speed settings until smooth & creamy.

Banana Strawberry & Kiwi Smoothie

Servings: About 2

INGREDIENTS

- 236.59 ml strawberry, frozen
- 2 frozen bananas, sliced
- 177.44 ml apple juice
- 236.59 ml kiwi

DIRECTIONS

- Place everything together in a high speed blender and blend on high speed settings until smooth & creamy.

Kiwi-Special Smoothie

Servings: About 2

INGREDIENTS

- 4 kiwi, peeled & sliced thinly
- 1 banana, medium
- 118.29 ml yogurt, plain & nonfat
- 2 tbsp. honey
- 1 tsp. lime juice
- 10 ice cubes

DIRECTIONS

- Put everything together (except 2 kiwi slices) in a high speed blender & blend on high speed settings until smooth. Serve in two large glasses & garnish each glass with a reserved kiwi slice.

Papaya Refreshment

Servings: About 2

INGREDIENTS

- 236.59 ml pineapple juice, chilled
- 118.29 ml banana, sliced
- 473.18 ml papayas, peeled, seeded & chopped
- 2 tsp. lime juice, fresh
- 118.29 ml milk
- 1 tbsp. honey
- 4 ice cubes

DIRECTIONS

- Put everything together in a high speed blender & blend until smooth & creamy. Serve in two large glasses.

Berry Papaya Smoothie

Servings: About 1

INGREDIENTS

- 236.59 ml berries, mixed & frozen
- 118.29 ml soymilk or skim milk
- 236.59 ml papaya, peeled & seeded
- 1 tbsp. honey

DIRECTIONS

- Put all of the ingredients in a high speed blender and blend on high settings until smooth.

Papaya Cherry Smoothie

A unique blend, you haven't tasted anything quite like it!

Servings: About 2

INGREDIENTS

- 236.59 ml papaya, peeled & diced
- 1 banana, large & frozen
- 473.18 ml big cherries, stemmed & pitted
- 1 tbsp. honey
- 354.88 ml white grape juice

DIRECTIONS

- Combine all of the ingredients together in a high speed blender. Blend on high settings until smooth and then pour the mixture into two large glasses & ENJOY!

Papaya Ginger Mint Smoothie

Papaya, ginger, mint, lemon juice…All immune-boosting powerhouse recipes.

Servings: About 4

INGREDIENTS

- 236.59 ml ice cube
- 1 tbsp. honey
- 591.47 ml papayas, chunks
- 16 mint leaves, fresh and 4 more sprigs for garnish
- 1 tbsp. ginger, fresh, peeled & finely chopped
- 158.51 ml yogurt, plain & nonfat
- Juice of 2 lemons

DIRECTIONS

- Refrigerate papaya for a minimum period of an hour or for overnight or until very cold.
- Add chilled papaya together with the yogurt, ice, honey, ginger, & lemon juice in a high speed blender. Blend on high settings.
- Add approximately 1/4 cup of water, 1 tbsp. at a time, until mixture is smooth and you get your desired consistency.
- Add in the mint leaves and blend again.
- Garnish with fresh mint sprigs.

Berry Kale Ginger Smoothie

It's suggested to boil kale lightly first before using it in any recipe, as the highly healthy ingredient is slightly toxic, however, when served raw.

Servings: About 1

INGREDIENTS

- 6 almonds
- 1 tbsp. lemon juice
- 6 berries, frozen
- 1 banana, medium
- 473.18 ml water
- 1/2" ginger
- 236.59 ml kale, tightly packed

DIRECTIONS

- Pack kale in two measuring cups. Add berries, splash of lemon juice, almonds & ginger. Fill the cup with water and blend either in Vitamix or in a high speed blender at high speed settings.
- Add in the banana & blend again, preferably at medium speed settings.

Green & Berry Smoothie

Servings: About 1

INGREDIENTS

- 236.59 ml each strawberry & cranberries
- Juice of 1 lemon or 1 lime
- 1 bunch wheat grass
- 236.59 ml spinach, roughly chopped
- 1/2 inch gingerroot, grated
- 1 cucumber with skin
- 236.59 ml broccoli
- Water

DIRECTIONS

- Wash every dry ingredient using cold water. Put approximately 60 ml of filtered water in a high speed blender.
- Add in the lime juice or lemon, cucumber, berries and then the leftover ingredients, preferably a small quantity at a time. Continue blending until smooth.

Spinach Broccoli & Strawberry Smoothie

Seems like an unusual combo, but it works.

Servings: About 1

INGREDIENTS

- 226.79 grams strawberry-apple juice, preferably Hansen's
- 1 banana, medium
- 236.59 ml strawberries, frozen
- 118.29 ml each broccoli & spinach

DIRECTIONS

- Add everything to a high speed blender and blend on high speed settings until smooth. Add ice and water until you get your desired thickness.

Classic Green Smoothie

Servings: About 12

INGREDIENTS

- 1 large carrot, chunks
- 1 kale leaf, large & with stem
- 8 pineapple, fresh & into chunks
- 1 crown large broccoli, chunks
- 1 cucumber, small & chunked (preferably 6" long)
- 236.59 ml water
- 1 apple, cored & quartered
- 1 orange, peeled & quartered

DIRECTIONS

- Starting with 120 ml of water; place everything together in a Vitamix and process until you get your desired consistency.

Fruit Delight Smoothie

Servings: About 1

INGREDIENTS

- 1 tbsp. wheat germ
- 59.14 ml blueberries, fresh & washed
- 1 banana, medium & cut into pieces, preferably 1"
- 3 tbsp. yogurt, low-fat & vanilla or plain
- 59.14 ml strawberries, fresh, washed & cut into small chunks
- 1 tbsp. honey
- 3 crushed ice cubes
- 1 sprig mint, fresh

DIRECTIONS

- Put everything in a high speed blender and blend approximately half a minute on liquefy speed.
- Pour into fluted or stemmed glass.
- Garnish with fresh mint. Serve & enjoy.

Blueberry Grape Juice Smoothie

Servings: About 1

INGREDIENTS

- 158.51 ml blueberries
- 2 tbsp. yogurt, plain
- 5 tbsp. white grape juice
- 1 sprig of mint, garnish
- 158.51 ml crushed ice,

DIRECTIONS

- Pulse everything together in a high speed blender until smooth.
- Transfer to a large glass and garnish with mint sprig at the top.

Delicious Berry Smoothie

Servings: About 4

INGREDIENTS

- 473.18 ml mixed berries, frozen (such as blueberry & strawberry)
- 1 sliced banana
- 236.59 ml yogurt, strawberry
- 1/2 tsp. white sugar
- 236.59 ml milk

DIRECTIONS

- Combine mixed berries together with the milk, banana, strawberry yogurt & sugar in a high speed blender.
- Cover & blend on high settings until smooth.
- Transfer the mixture into four glasses & serve.

Ginger Berry Smoothie

Servings: About 2

INGREDIENTS

- 28.39 ml flax seed, ground
- 1 tbsp. ginger, fresh
- 236.59 ml berries, frozen
- 1 banana, large
- 354.88 ml water, to taste

DIRECTIONS

- Puree everything together in a high speed blender until smooth, on high speed settings.
- Transfer the mixture into two large glasses & enjoy!

Veggie & Frozen Fruit Smoothie

Servings: About 1

INGREDIENTS

- 236.59 ml Baby Spinach, fresh
- 1 banana, small
- 118.29 ml berries, frozen such as blackberries, blueberries & raspberries
- 2 tbsp. Splenda or to taste
- 236.59 ml frozen watermelon pieces
- 118.29 ml ice, crushed
- 1 tsp. honey

DIRECTIONS

- Blend banana, frozen fruits, & ice using a regular blender or an immersion blender until smooth.
- Add in a small quantity of spinach at a time to the blender and thoroughly blend after every addition.
- Sweeten the smoothie to taste & serve immediately.

Refreshing Strawberry Smoothie

Servings: About 1

INGREDIENTS

- 118.29 ml yogurt, plain & low-fat
- 118.29 ml berries, frozen
- Cheerios toasted oat cereal
- 118.29 ml milk

DIRECTIONS

- Add berries together with the yogurt and milk in a high speed blender and blend on high settings.
- Transfer the mixture into a glass & for a pre-biotic crunch; top it with Cherrios cereal.

Spinach Smoothie

Servings: About 2

INGREDIENTS

- 1 peeled apple, granny smith or golden delicious
- 226.79 grams spinach or Kale or Arugula, fresh or frozen
- 1 banana, medium
- 236.59 ml water
- 1 orange, peeled

DIRECTIONS

- Peel & slice the fruit. Add the sliced fruit to a high speed blender and blend on high settings until reasonably smooth.
- You may add a small quantity of sweetener or maple syrup to taste, if you find the taste is too tart.

Berries Kale Spinach Smoothie

Servings: About 1

INGREDIENTS

- 236.59 ml kale
- 236.59 ml orange juice
- 236.59 ml spinach
- 236.59 ml mixed berries, frozen

DIRECTIONS

- Add everything in the blender's container and blend on high settings until smooth. Transfer the mixture to a large glass & enjoy.

Andrea's Amazing Green Drink

The secret ingredient is the parsley.

Servings: About 4

INGREDIENTS

- 2 cored apples
- 1 to 2 cucumbers, medium
- 1 celery stalk
- 473.18 ml spinach
- 1 bunch parsley, chopped
- Juice of 1/2 lemon
- 1 tsp. gingerroot, 1/2"
- Juice of 1 lime
- 113.39 grams mineral water or ice cubes, handful

Optional ingredients

- Banana, medium
- Fruit juice, unsweetened
- Carrot, raw

DIRECTIONS

- Put everything together in a high speed blender & blend on high settings until smooth; you may even use a juicer. You may need to add more of water, if it's very thick.
- To make the green drink sweetens; you may try adding other items such as Splenda or Honey.

Kale Orange & Watermelon Smoothie

Servings: About 5

INGREDIENTS

- 150 grams kale
- 80 grams spinach
- 1/4 whole watermelon
- 3 oranges, large
- 1 lemon
- Mint, fresh & chopped
- 1 tbsp. flax seeds, ground
- 2 tbsp. coconut oil

DIRECTIONS

- Heat water in a large saucepan until boiling and let the kale & spinach to steam approximately five minutes, let them cool at room temperature.
- Chop up all the ingredients & blend the fruit in a high speed blender with a small quantity of water.
- Add the leftover ingredients.

Devil Green Smoothie

Servings: About 1

INGREDIENTS

- 1 banana, medium & frozen
- 118.29 ml Greek yogurt
- 473.18 ml spinach, raw
- 118.29 ml ice
- 122 ml coconut milk, 0.5can

DIRECTIONS

- Put everything together in a high speed blender and blend on high settings until smooth and creamy.

Quinoa Spinach/Kale Smoothie

You can put quinoa in a smoothie? What's the world coming to?!

Servings: About 1

INGREDIENTS

- 473.18 ml kale or spinach
- 236.59 ml grapes, green
- 177.44 ml banana, frozen & sliced
- 118.29 ml kiwi, chopped
- 3 tbsp. quinoa
- 236.59 ml orange juice

DIRECTIONS

- Put everything in a high speed blender and blend until smooth. Pour the mixture into large glass.

Spinach Apple Smoothie

Servings: About 1

INGREDIENTS

- 473.18 ml spinach
- 1 apple, small & cut up into small chunks
- 236.59 ml milk, non dairy or almond & soy
- 1 banana, small & frozen
- ½ tsp. cinnamon

DIRECTIONS

- Put everything together into a high speed blender and blend on high settings (you may add a couple of ice cubes; if you don't have a frozen banana).
- Whiz & enjoy.

Tropical Smoothie

Servings: About 8

INGREDIENTS

- 354.88 ml skim milk
- 2 mangoes & 2 papayas, preferably peeled, seeded & chopped
- 177.44 ml orange juice, freshly squeezed
- 3 bananas, ripe & medium
- 354.88 ml water
- 177.44 ml yogurt, nonfat
- 1419.54 ml ice
- 1 tbsp. honey

DIRECTIONS

- Mix 120 ml of mango together with 1 banana, 240 ml papaya, 120 ml milk, 60 ml orange juice, 1 tsp. honey, 60 ml yogurt , 475 ml ice and 120 ml water in a high speed blender & blend until smooth.
- Repeat the process until you have utilized all of the ingredients.
- Serve & enjoy!

Strawberry Papaya Soymilk Smoothie

Servings: About 3

INGREDIENTS

- 236.59 ml papaya, chopped & chilled
- 118.29 ml chilled orange juice
- 236.59 ml soymilk, vanilla-flavored
- 2 tbsp. soy protein concentrate, powdered
- 118.29 ml strawberries, unsweetened & frozen
- 1 tbsp. honey

DIRECTIONS

- Combine soymilk together with the orange juice in a high speed blender; add in the strawberries, papaya, honey & protein powder. Cover & blend on high settings until smooth.

Banana Papaya Smoothie

Servings: About 2

INGREDIENTS

- 158.51 ml orange juice
- 2 bananas, peeled & sliced ½" thick
- 236.59 ml papaya, preferably peeled, seeded & diced

DIRECTIONS

- Place papaya and bananas in a reseal able plastic bag, preferably in a single layer; place in a freezer for a minimum period of an hour.
- Place the frozen fruit in a high speed blender. Add in the orange juice & puree until smooth.
- Pour into two glasses & enjoy.

Papaya & Coconut Milk Smoothie

Servings: About 4

INGREDIENTS

- 177.44 ml coconut milk
- 2 tsp. vanilla extract
- 1 to 2 lime juice & zest
- 1 papaya, preferably peeled, seeded & cubed (approximately 560 grams)
- 2 tbsp. turbinado sugar

DIRECTIONS

- Place everything together in a high speed blender & blend on high settings until smooth.
- Transfer the mixture into four glasses & garnish each glass with the lime slices.

Pineapple Papaya Smoothie

Servings: About 2

INGREDIENTS

- 236.59 ml papaya, frozen & into small chunks
- 3⁄4 tsp. ginger, ground
- 118.29 ml yogurt, plain & nonfat
- 236.59 ml pineapple juice

DIRECTIONS

- Puree everything together in a high speed blender until smooth.

Lime Papaya Mango Smoothie

Servings: About 2

INGREDIENTS

- 118.29 ml papaya, peeled & chopped
- 1 dash vanilla extract, raw
- 236.59 ml nut milk
- 3 tbsp. lime juice, fresh
- 118.29 ml mango, peeled & chopped

DIRECTIONS

- Mix everything together in a high speed blender and blend on high settings until smooth & creamy.

Healthy For Tummy Smoothie

Servings: About 1

INGREDIENTS

- 1 banana, medium & frozen
- 236.59 ml yoghurt (soy, Greek or of your choice)
- 118.29 ml each cranberries & blueberries
- 1 papaya, small
- 236.59 ml chamomile tea (cold)

DIRECTIONS

- Put everything together in a high speed blender & blend on high settings until smooth & creamy.

Tempting Kale & Berries Smoothie

Servings: About 2

INGREDIENTS

- 118.29 ml coconut milk
- 3 ice cubes
- 118.29 ml water
- 60 ml blueberries, frozen
- 2 strawberries
- 354.88 ml kale, only leaves
- 1/2 banana, frozen
- 60 ml papaya, chunks
- agave nectar or honey

DIRECTIONS

- Add kale together with the water & ice cubes in a high speed blender until smooth and then add in the remaining ingredients.
- Add more of honey and water for desired sweetness & consistency.

Fruit Delight Smoothie

Servings: About 2

INGREDIENTS

- 1 tbsp. orange juice
- 226.79 grams vanilla yogurt, approximately 1 carton
- 1 tsp. brown sugar, packed
- 473.18 ml strawberries, unsweetened, frozen & partially thawed
- 1 tsp. lemon juice
- 1 and 1/2 tsp. honey
- 1 tsp. granulated sugar

DIRECTIONS

- Combine everything together in a high speed blender & blend on high settings until smooth.
- Transfer the mixture into glasses, preferably chilled & serve immediately.

Vanilla Strawberry Smoothie

Servings: About 2

INGREDIENTS

- 236.59 ml milk
- 1 and 1/2 tsp. lemon juice
- 59.14 ml vanilla yogurt
- 1 and 1/2 tsp. honey
- 473.18 ml strawberries, fresh
- 2 to 3 tbsp. sugar
- 10 ice cubes

DIRECTIONS

- Place everything together in a blender and blend until ice is completely crushed.
- Transfer into frozen mason jar or mug & enjoy

Mouthwatering Raspberry Smoothie

Servings: About 4

INGREDIENTS

- 118.29 ml raspberry yogurt
- 1/2 bag raspberries, frozen
- 354.88 ml milk
- 1 tsp. lemon juice
- 5 tbsp. sugar
- 16 ice cubes or 1 ice cube tray

DIRECTIONS

- Blend all of the ingredients together in a blender until combined completely.
- Ensure that the raspberries & ice cubes are crushed completely.
- Enjoy

Kiwifruit Frappe

Servings: About 2

INGREDIENTS

- 236.59 ml kiwi fruit, peeled & chopped
- 118.29 ml pineapple, chopped
- 354.88 ml ice cubes
- 1 tbsp. lemon juice
- 236.59 ml apple juice, unsweetened

DIRECTIONS

- Arrange two large glasses in a fridge and let them chill for couple of hours.
- Add everything together in a high speed blender and blend until smooth.
- Pour the mixture into the chilled glasses.
- Garnish with kiwifruit slice.
- Serve immediately.

Raspberry Sipper

Servings: About 4

INGREDIENTS

- 354.88 ml raspberry sherbet
- 295.73 ml white grape juice, unsweetened
- 1 tbsp. lemon juice
- 59.14 ml water
- 10 ice cubes
- 295.73 ml raspberries, fresh
- Mint sprigs, fresh

DIRECTIONS

- Combine grape juice and the raspberries in a high speed blender and process on high settings until smooth.
- Extract the liquid as much as possible by straining the mixture.
- Combine the sherbet together with the liquid, lemon juice and water in a blender & blend again until smooth.
- Add in the ice cubes & process until frothy.
- Pour into four equal glasses and if desired, garnish with fresh mint sprigs.
- Serve immediately

Orange Juice & Cranberry Slushee

Servings: About 4

INGREDIENTS

- 59.14 ml orange juice
- 3 cloves
- 1 tbsp. lemon or lime juice
- 59.14 to 78.07 ml sugar
- 1 pint cranberries
- 473.18 ml water

DIRECTIONS

- Add cranberries in water & cook approximately five minutes, until the skin of the cranberries pop open.
- Using cheesecloth; strain and bring the juice to boil & add in the cloves and sugar. Cook approximately two more minutes; cool at room temperature.
- Add lime or lemon juice and orange juice. Pour the mixture to your desired glasses and let them chill thoroughly in a freezer.
- If desired, garnish your drink with orange slices, preferably fresh.

Watermelon Strawberry Slushy

Servings: About 5

INGREDIENTS

- 473.18 ml ice cubes
- 78.07 ml lemon juice
- 1 pint strawberries, fresh & halved
- 78.07 ml granulated sugar
- 473.18 ml watermelon, cubed & seeded

DIRECTIONS

- Combine everything together (except the ice cubes) in a high speed blender and blend on high settings until smooth.
- Gradually add in the ice cubes and continue blending until you get a slushy form.
- Serve immediately

Berry Cherry Smoothie

Hey, that rhymes.

Servings: About 2

INGREDIENTS

- 236.59 ml dark sweet cherry, unsweetened, frozen & pitted
- 2 tbsp. honey
- 236.59 ml cranberry juice, chilled
- 1 tbsp. lemon juice
- 118.29 ml red raspberries, frozen & lightly sweetened

DIRECTIONS

- Combine everything together in a high speed blender. Cover & blend on high settings until smooth

Blue & Black Berries Smoothie

Servings: About 1

INGREDIENTS

- 236.59 ml soda water
- 1 tsp lemon juice
- 78.07 ml blackberry
- 2 tbsp. honey
- 158.51 ml blueberries

DIRECTIONS

- Put everything together in a high speed blender and blend on high settings until smooth.

Immune System Mega Smoothie

I told you this recipe book was worth buying. If you follow this recipe and drink it often, you'll be the healthiest guy / gal you know.

Servings: About 1

INGREDIENTS

- 1 celery stalk
- 118.29 ml cucumber
- 1 apple, cored
- 354.88 ml spinach
- 1 tsp. ginger, fresh
- 118.29 ml parsley
- 1 and 1/2 tbsp. lime juice
- 1 tbsp. flax seed oil
- 59.14 ml sparkling water
- 1 and 1/2 tbsp. lemon juice

DIRECTIONS

- Chop up every dry ingredient, preferably into uniform pieces & then add them in a high speed blender. Cover & blend on high settings until smooth

Broccoli Carrot Smoothie

Servings: About 2

INGREDIENTS

- 236.59 ml orange juice
- 2 mandarin orange sections
- 473.18 ml spinach leaves
- 4 broccoli florets, chopped
- 1 carrot, chopped

DIRECTIONS

- Blend all the fruits and vegetables together until smooth. Pour the mixture into two glasses and refrigerate for an hour. Serve cold

Apple Juice Carrot Smoothie

Servings: About 2

INGREDIENTS

- 354.88 ml apple juice
- 177.44 ml boiling water
- 3 medium carrots, peeled and sliced

DIRECTIONS

- Cook carrots, in 180 ml of boiling water approximately 20 minutes in a small saucepan, covered.
- Cool at room temperature.
- Put the cooked carrot together with the apple juice in a high speed blender.
- Cover; blend on high settings until the carrots are smooth.
- If required, you may add more of apple juice to get your desired consistency.
- Chill & serve

Kale Carrot & Apple Juice

Servings: About 1

INGREDIENTS

- 78.07 ml parsley
- 2 kale leaves
- 3 carrots
- 1 apple, stem & seeds removed
- 2 celery ribs
- Honey or Splenda

DIRECTIONS

- Wash & cut every vegetable and put them in a juicer, preferably one by one. You may add honey or Splenda later on, if you don't like the taste and mix well.

Tomato & Carrot Smoothie

Servings: About 2

INGREDIENTS

- 1 celery stalk, chopped into pieces, preferably ½"
- 4 carrots, medium & cut into cubes, preferably 1"
- 1 tsp. black pepper, freshly grounded
- 6 tomatoes, medium & quartered
- 2 tbsp. lemon juice, fresh
- ice cube, as per your needs
- Salt to taste

DIRECTIONS

- Freeze the chopped carrots & tomatoes approximately half an hour.
- Add the frozen chopped tomato cubes in a smoothie maker or in a high speed blender and blend.
- Toss in the carrot cubes & blend again.
- Add in the celery pieces, pepper and salt and blend again.
- Gradually add in the ice cubes & lemon juice; blend again.
- Pour the juice into a glass, preferably long stemmed & serve chilled.
- Enjoy

Totally Red Smoothie

Carrots and beets creates a blood-like drink that will likely raise eyebrows from your roommates.

Servings: About 4

INGREDIENTS

- 1 beet medium & fresh (approximately 170.09 grams)
- 2 tbsp. ground flax seeds
- 1 carrot, medium & fresh (approximately 113.39 grams)
- Juice of 1 lime
- 1 apple, medium & fresh (approximately 170.09 grams)
- 1 banana, frozen or fresh
- 907.18 grams water
- 1 tbsp. ginger, fresh & grated
- 1 tbsp. Chia seeds
- 1 tbsp. hemp seeds

DIRECTIONS

- Put everything into your high speed blender container and process on high settings until smooth.
- Transfer the mixture into four glasses and put them in a fridge for a minimum period of half an hour and then serve.

Tropical Mean Green Smoothie

A mean, green end to this book. I hope you found these smoothie recipes beneficial for the long-term. This particular smoothie is one of my favorites.

Servings: About 2

INGREDIENTS

- 118.29 ml almond milk
- 2 mandarin oranges, peeled
- 78.07 ml pineapple chunk
- 1 banana, small
- 236.59 ml spinach leaves
- 1 celery stalk
- 59.14 ml parsley, fresh
- 1 carrot, medium
- 1/2 tsp. real vanilla
- 1 tbsp. Chia seeds

DIRECTIONS

- Use pineapple chunks (fresh) & bananas (frozen) and cut them into small pieces.
- Add all the veggies & fruit to a high speed blender such as Blendtec or Vitamix.
- Add in the almond milk and blend on high settings until smooth.
- Enjoy.

A Message from Andrea

Thank you so much for taking the time to read this book. I hope that this was of some benefit to you.

You can find many more books like this one I've created by checking out my Amazon page at the following address: http://www.amazon.com/Andrea-Silver/e/B00W820AR6/.

You can also get in touch with me personally at AndreaSilverWellness@gmail.com if you have any questions or ideas.

33033789R00149

Printed in Great Britain
by Amazon